Smart Money, Broke Mindset

Why Smart People Get Stuck With Money — And How to Break the Loop

IP Buquiron

IP Buquiron Press

ISBN 978-1-0694591-5-2 (paperback)
ISBN 978-1-0694591-0-7 (ebook)

Disclaimer

This book provides general information about money, behavior, and decision-making. It is not intended as financial, legal, tax, investment, or medical advice. Readers should consult qualified professionals for advice specific to their situation.

AI writing tools were used during the development, editing, and refinement of this book under the author's direction and supervision. The author reviewed, revised, and takes full responsibility for the final content.

First edition, 2026

Published independently by
IP Buquiron Press
Toronto, Ontario, Canada

Dedication

To my parents, Medying and Luis,
who raised us with so little — and so much faith.

Contents

A Note on the Narratives

The illustrative characters and scenes throughout this book are drawn from real behavioral patterns, professional observations, and insights gathered across many individuals and situations. They are used to illuminate ideas and concepts, not to document any single person's life. The characters are composites, not case studies, and are not intended to portray any specific person. Names, identifying details, circumstances, and sequences have been changed, combined, or reconstructed for clarity and illustration.

Personal scenes from my own life are reconstructed from memory and reflect the emotional truth of the experiences as I lived them. The wider reflections in this book also draw on insights from my decades-long career as a Professional Engineer, where work across countries, projects, and systems taught me to pay attention to judgment, risk, verification, responsibility, and the gap between what people know and what they are able to do under pressure.

Introduction

"Being smart isn't the problem. It's the trap."

2:47 a.m. Again.

You're lying there with your phone, thumb hovering over the banking app. Already checked twice tonight, but maybe—just maybe—the numbers changed.

They haven't. They never do.

The balance stares back. Not terrible, but not enough. Never enough for someone who's supposed to be the smart one, right?

Your chest tightens. That familiar knot.

You close the app fast. Like someone's watching.

Then it starts—that voice in your head: God, you should have this figured out by now. You run presentations at work. You solve actual problems. Why can't you just get this?

So you make the promise. Tomorrow. Tomorrow you'll finally sort this mess out.

But when tomorrow comes? You'll spend an hour researching whether YNAB or another budgeting app is better instead of just opening your credit card statement.

If your chest has ever tightened at a number on a screen, you already know: money was never about math. It's always been about identity.

That cycle you just lived—the one that feels so personal, so shameful? It has a name. And once you see it, you can break it.

Why Smart Minds Stall With Money

Picture this: marketing directors juggling six-figure ad budgets who forget to pay $25 utility bills. Not because they're broke—because they spent two weeks overanalyzing budgeting apps instead of simply paying the bill.

When you're smart, you solve problems by thinking harder. Can't figure out the presentation? Think more. Complex project falling apart? Analyze deeper. Works everywhere else. Naturally, you apply the same strategy to money.

Here's where most advice misses the mark: more thinking does not equal better financial results.

Money is rarely solved by thinking alone—it's mostly a doing problem. The more you think, the more paralyzed you become.

Here's the paradox: the very skills that power your work—pattern-spotting, optimization, scenario-building—can backfire when money is involved. When outcomes are uncertain and emotional, more analysis doesn't create action. It delays it.

If that last sentence made you want to argue with me, you're exactly who this book is for. The resistance you're feeling? That's your analytical brain trying to solve this problem by thinking harder about thinking harder. Notice it. We'll work with that resistance, not against it.

The Pattern You've Been Running

A few years ago, I caught myself four days into "researching" the best high-yield savings account. Four days comparing interest rates that differed by 0.15 percent—roughly $7.50 on a $5,000 balance over a year.

What was I actually avoiding? Opening my credit card statement to see how much I'd spent that month. The "research" gave me permission to delay the discomfort. Better yet, it made me feel productive while procrastinating.

Standing there at 11 p.m. on the fourth night, seventeen browser tabs open comparing APYs, I finally saw it. My analytical brain wasn't helping me—it was protecting me from something I didn't want to face.

If structural factors—low wages, medical or family costs, immigration or credential limits—are constraining your options, that's real, not a mindset failure. This book works within your current constraints while building capacity over time.

The Smart Struggle Loop™

This pattern has a name. Once you see it, you can interrupt it.

Your analytical mind—the same one that makes you successful at work—becomes the trap that keeps you financially stuck. The Smart Struggle Loop operates as a self-reinforcing cycle:

You notice a money problem → Anxiety demands immediate solution → You research extensively instead of acting → Research feels productive, delaying real action → The loop repeats. The problem remains.

The sharper your mind is, the easier it becomes to keep thinking instead of moving. Understanding this pattern changes everything.

Suddenly your financial struggles aren't personal failures—they're predictable patterns you can interrupt.

Once you can name the Loop, you can see why typical advice rarely sticks. That's the gap this book closes.

What Makes This Book Different

Most financial advice tells you to budget harder. This book teaches you to think differently about why budgeting feels impossible in the first place.

The typical advice assumes you need more discipline. Smart people often need less thinking, not more willpower.

As a structural engineer born in the Philippines who built my international career across multiple countries—Saudi Arabia, Singapore, and Canada—I know analytical precision. I also know it fails spectacularly when applied to emotional complexity.

I grew up outside the usual centers of privilege in the Philippines and earned my engineering degree from a public university. Although I became a licensed Professional Engineer in the Philippines in 1988, my professional journey truly took flight in 1992 when I began my career in Saudi Arabia, moving to Singapore in 1995 before immigrating to Canada in 2003. When I arrived, my Philippine license wasn't enough—I had to prove my competence all over again to earn my P.Eng. in Ontario. That experience of being credentialed yet starting over taught me about the gap between capability and recognition.

Years later, I discovered the same analytical paralysis operating at every income level. The marketing director earning $120,000 felt the same paralysis I'd felt at $32,000 when I first arrived in Canada. Different numbers, identical trap.

Money makes you feel like a complete fraud. Like you're faking adulthood while everyone else got the manual. Research investment strategies for three months without buying a single stock. Overthink a thirty-dollar restaurant choice while your retirement account sits empty. The intelligence that solves problems everywhere else somehow can't solve this one.

Why Information Alone Isn't Enough

If you've ever tried to think your way to perfect certainty, you already know why the usual tips fall flat. [1] They solve for information, not for action under emotion.

Here's the disconnect: most financial guidance treats money like a pure math problem. Save 20 percent. Cut expenses. Invest in index funds.

But money isn't just math for smart people. It's tangled up with identity, self-worth, and the stories we tell ourselves about what we deserve.

You already know what to do—read the books, understand compound interest, set a budget. The problem isn't knowledge—it's the gap between knowing and doing. That gap is where the cycle lives.

Traditional approaches assume you need more information. You don't. What you need are different tools for the emotional complexity that makes money decisions hard.

---

1. Barry Schwartz, The Paradox of Choice: Why More Is Less (New York: Ecco, 2004).

Advice vs Recognition

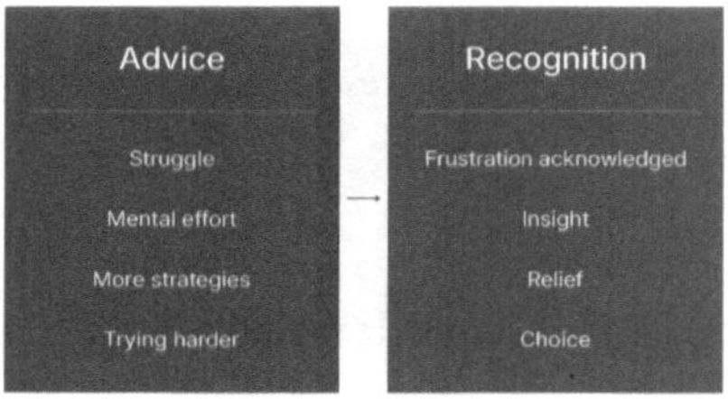

Effort tries to fix the problem. Recognition dissolves it.

The identity you've built your entire life around—being "the smart one"—becomes the very thing that traps you.

The Hidden Cost of Being "The Smart One"

Growing up smart comes with expectations. Figure things out faster. Make better decisions. Avoid obvious mistakes.

These expectations become internal pressure. When money feels confusing or overwhelming, the shame hits harder because you should know better.

You end up hiding financial struggles because admitting confusion feels like admitting you're not as smart as everyone thinks.

So you suffer in silence. Research solutions instead of implementing them. Analyze problems instead of solving them.

What Smart People Actually Need

Smart people don't need a different personality—you need a setup that respects how your brain works. Elegant simplicity over complexity. Three options instead of thirty. Permission to act on 70 percent certainty rather than waiting for perfect information. The clarity to see the next step without overthinking every possibility.

The same pattern recognition that makes you good at your job can identify when you're stuck in financial loops. The same systematic thinking that solves complex problems can create simple action triggers that bypass emotional resistance.

A Note Before We Begin

This book is designed for readers whose money struggles are shaped by patterns, pressure, behavior, identity, or decision-making within ordinary financial life. If you're facing an urgent situation—such as losing housing, going without food, facing legal action, medical debt, unsafe debt pressure, or any crisis requiring immediate support—seek local help first through a qualified financial adviser, legal aid service, community support agency, government office, crisis line, or trusted professional in your area.

There is no shame in that order. Stabilize the emergency first. The work in this book will be more useful once immediate safety is in place.

How to Use This Book

This book moves through four parts, each preparing the next.

Part One: Recognition. You learn to see the Smart Struggle Loop through your money story, your nervous system, and the beliefs running below conscious thought.

Part Two: Earning. You learn to see your existing skills as monetizable value and build income that generates reliably.

Part Three: Managing. You automate money flow, build wealth, eliminate debt through system design, and protect what you've built.

Part Four: Living. You regulate the stress that persists even after systems work, and design a life money serves rather than controls.

You don't need to read this perfectly. If you're in an immediate financial crisis, start with Chapters 1, 2, and 9—recognition, interruption, and building more stable money systems—then return to the full sequence when you have room. If you want the complete progression, read straight through; each part prepares the next. If you're already managing reasonably well, the recognition and identity work in Part One may give you the clearest insight, while the systems chapters can reinforce what you already have in place.

Between some chapters you will find short interludes. They're not summaries or assignments. They are pauses—a moment to notice what is happening in you as the work becomes more personal. Read them once, let them do their job, and continue.

Where This Journey Begins

These are not separate tools you pick up at random. They build on each other.

Chapter 1 shows you the money story already shaping your decisions. What follows gives you the tools to interrupt that pattern, build systems that reduce friction, and create a life money can support rather than control.

That progression matters. You can't build sustainable income approaches if you're still trapped in analysis paralysis. You can't create calmer money systems if limiting beliefs and old body responses keep hijacking your decisions. Each part prepares the way for the next.

The loop does not begin with a bad decision.

It begins the moment intelligence turns on itself—and calls the turning productive.

PART ONE: RECOGNITION

This is where the pattern becomes visible.

Before money can change, the Loop that turns intelligence into delay has to be named clearly enough to interrupt.

Chapter 1: Your Money Story Is Running the Show

Jennifer was a data analyst. She built financial models for her company's multimillion-dollar marketing campaigns. She knew how to organize complexity, weigh risk, and prepare for decisions most people would avoid.

Jennifer had the spreadsheet ready before the loan officer said a word.

Forty-seven rows. Twenty-three criteria, color-coded by weight. She knew how to prepare.

The loan officer slid the application across the desk. One page. Six fields.

Jennifer's hand didn't move.

She sat there four minutes. She could feel the spreadsheet behind her eyes—all that preparation—and underneath it, the real problem: she had modeled every scenario except the one where she said yes.

She had been planning the bakery for three years. Sketching layouts on napkins during lunch breaks. Testing recipes on friends who kept telling her to stop talking about it and open the shop already.

The numbers were solid. The demand was there. Her accountant had looked over the projections and nodded.

But the moment the plan required borrowed money, her body stopped reading it as a business decision. It read it as danger.

Her hand shook over the signature line. The pen felt heavy. Dad's voice cut through everything: "Money destroys families."

Jennifer left without signing.

That night, she opened her laptop to "research alternatives." Three hours later, her credit card statement still sat unopened in another tab. Six days old.

The spreadsheet on her second monitor: Forty-seven rows. Twenty-three criteria, color-coded and formula-driven.

Perfect.

She still hadn't opened that credit card statement.

The real trigger was never the budgeting app. It was her father's fist on the table. Her mother crying over the bank statement. The lesson an eight-year-old absorbs before she has any way to question it.

Her hand trembles as she finally clicks the credit card tab. There it is—$8,947 staring back at her like an accusation. Her heart hammers, her palms slick with cold sweat, and her breath catches before she can remind herself that she is no longer eight years old.

If this scene hits close to home, take a breath. You can skim if you need to. We'll be here when you're ready.

"Money destroys families," he'd snarled, voice cracking with desperation she didn't understand until decades later.

Jennifer's midnight research spiral isn't about budgeting apps. It's about a pattern learned at eight that still controls her financial life at thirty-four. That's her money story executing.

It left a belief deep in eight-year-old Jennifer. She couldn't name it then, but she felt it in her bones: money destroys families.

This is your money story executing in real time. Invisible childhood programming overriding conscious adult choice.

How Your Money Story Takes Over

The same analytical loop that kept her circling those budgeting tabs was shaped by the money story she learned at eight.

Jennifer's experience reveals how your money story operates through four predictable stages:

The script was "Money destroys families," burned in at age eight during Dad's breakdown.

The trigger? Loan applications, investment opportunities, anything involving financial growth.

The behavior was avoidance—flee, freeze, shut down.

The reward? False safety from "dangerous" financial growth.

Your money story activates the same internal cycle — just triggered by your specific childhood programming.

If any of this sounds familiar, you're not alone.

Research in neuroscience on how fear is encoded and retrieved—including Joseph LeDoux's foundational work on emotional memory—suggests that emotionally charged childhood experiences can create automatic response patterns that persist for decades. A child's mind does not evaluate those moments the way an adult mind can.[1]

Think about your own money weirdness. Why does your chest tighten at certain numbers? Why do you freeze making specific financial decisions? That's your money story activating.

Awareness itself is the first interruption.

External constraints are real. But internal patterns still shape how decisions are made within them.

The 2 a.m. Money Check

Before we go deeper into how these patterns form, let's identify if you're running them right now.

Quick test: How many times this month have you checked your bank balance after midnight? Refreshed your brokerage account during anxiety spirals? Opened and closed your budget app without making any changes?

If the answer is more than zero, you're running automated money patterns below conscious awareness. These aren't character flaws. They're learned responses your nervous system executes automatically when triggered.

My Singapore Lesson (The $180 Paralysis)

I learned about invisible money programming the hard way during my engineering career in Singapore.

Standing in a bookstore for forty-five minutes, paralyzed over a $180 technical manual I needed for work. Behind me, other shoppers tossed items in their baskets without hesitation. And there I stood, frozen, unable to buy a book.

My rational brain knew I could afford it. I had money in my account. But the programming from the scarcity I grew up with—where

$180 represented weeks of family income—had become a prison I couldn't escape even after my circumstances changed.

My wife and I had agreed to live on bare essentials while building our careers in Singapore, but this wasn't conscious budgeting. This was survival programming that once helped my family stretch every peso now sabotaging my professional growth.

While other shoppers moved freely, I finally saw it: This wasn't about the money. It was about the programming.

You're not lazy. You're not bad with money. You've been running learned patterns that once served a purpose but now limit your possibilities.

Different stories, same code: fear learned early keeps rerunning until you see it.

Where Money Patterns Begin

Your money story was programmed early, often before you had any way to question it. It usually takes shape through four channels.

Family Scripts taught you what money meant. Phrases like "We can't afford that" or "Money doesn't grow on trees" rarely felt situational to a child. They felt true.

Money Wounds turned emotionally charged moments into lasting instructions. Jennifer's kitchen table moment was one. Your own may still live in your body.

Cultural Messages taught you what people like you were supposed to do with money—whether to save, share, fear it, distrust it, or never expect much from it.

Modeled Behaviors showed you how adults actually handled pressure, regardless of what they said. Your nervous system recorded those lessons long before you could evaluate them.

The Patterns Driving Your Money Decisions

Most people run some variation of five common patterns.

The avoider learned that money equals danger or shame, so looking directly at it feels threatening. The hoarder learned that safety requires constant vigilance, so spending feels risky even when the numbers say otherwise.

The overgiver learned that worth comes from providing for others, so their own stability keeps getting outranked. The denier learned that ignorance feels safer than clarity, so problems stay hidden until they grow larger.

The perfectionist learned that safety requires total control, so action keeps getting delayed until everything feels perfect.

You may see yourself in more than one. Most people do. If you recognized pieces of yourself here, that's not failure. It's pattern recognition.

Where the Loop Hooks You

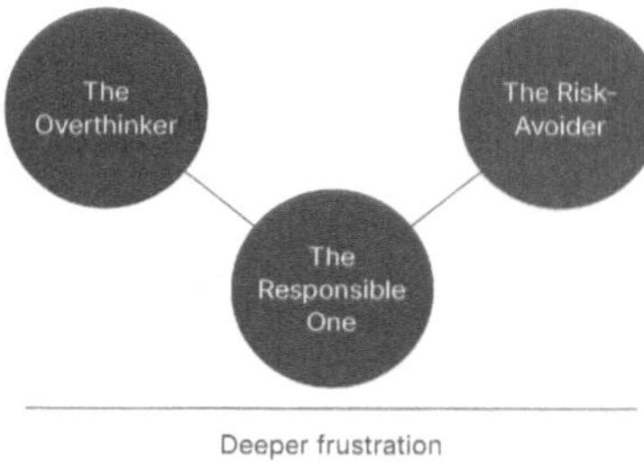

Different entry points. The same trap.

The Voice Test

Next time you're about to spend money on something you want (not need), listen to the voice in your head. Whose voice is it? Your dad warning about scarcity? Your mom's guilt about "wasting" money? Your culture's judgment about "people like us" not deserving nice things?

That voice isn't you. It's your downloaded programming. And once you can hear it separately from your actual thoughts, you begin to see it as learned code, not immutable truth.

When you recognize your money story activating, you're catching the Smart Struggle Loop mid-launch. That awareness is the first interruption point.

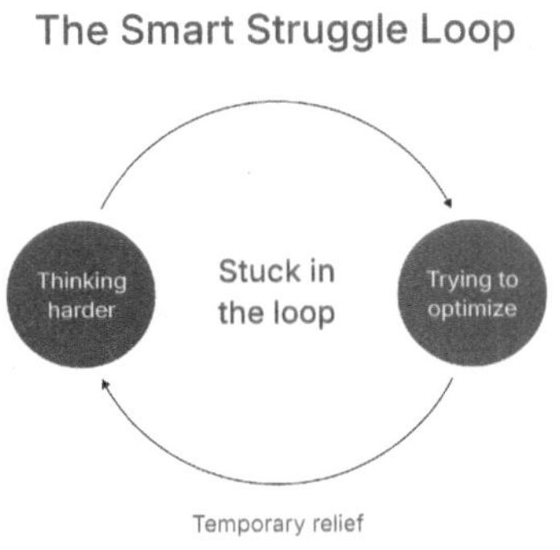

Why effort alone keeps repeating the same results.

What Recognition Reveals

Once you see your money story clearly, certain things become visible that were invisible before.

Observation alone weakens a pattern's grip. The pattern starts losing power when you stop mistaking it for something you can't see.

People notice which core pattern they're running. The physical response gives it away. When you think about money, what happens in your body? Chest tightness, stomach drop, jaw clench? That sensation has a history. When did you first feel this exact feeling around money? What was happening? The pattern usually has a name: "Money is dangerous." "I don't deserve to spend." "Financial success makes me a bad person."

Specific situations that activate the pattern become obvious. Which money moments trigger your stress response? Opening bills? Salary negotiations? Investment decisions? Checking your bank balance? Looking at price tags? If you freeze when opening bills, your money story probably involves shame or fear of scarcity. If you panic during negotiations, it might connect to worthiness or conflict avoidance.

The automatic behaviors start standing out. How do you sabotage yourself when triggered? Do you "forget" to send invoices? Procrastinate financial decisions through endless research? Buy things impulsively to avoid larger money conversations? Thomas the graphic designer realized he'd built an entire business model around avoiding price conversations. His underpricing wasn't generosity—it was automated conflict avoidance. Your avoidance is probably more sophisticated than you realize. Look for the patterns where you're "helping" others while sabotaging yourself.

What the pattern was protecting becomes clearer. What does this pattern provide? Safety? Identity? Belonging? This is the hardest part to see because the payoff feels necessary, even though it's costing you everything. Henry's hoarding protected him from ever experiencing his mother's shock when the business failed. His anxiety was the price of that protection. Rachel's overgiving kept her valuable and loved.

Her depletion was the price of belonging. What would you lose if you changed your money patterns? That fear reveals what your current programming is protecting.

The relationship between your old beliefs and current reality becomes visible. Jennifer's new understanding wasn't "Money is wonderful." It was "Money amplifies whatever values I already hold. Dad's desperation wasn't caused by money—it revealed existing family dysfunction." That recognition—seeing the difference between inherited fear and current truth—is where the pattern starts to lose its automatic grip.

How Jennifer's Pattern Shifted

Six months after recognizing her pattern, Jennifer signed her business loan with hands that still trembled.

That signature did not make the business easy, but it made the business possible.

Turns out her father's "money destroys families" explosion wasn't about money. It was a desperate man's situational crisis during a recession that cost him his job, not a universal truth about wealth.

Eight-year-old Jennifer had absorbed his situational despair as universal truth.

Jennifer's New Understanding: "Money amplifies positive impact."

Today, Jennifer's bakery employs twelve people. Her morning regulars became friends who gather for coffee and conversation. She sponsors the community center's after-school program.

The money didn't corrupt her. It amplified her values.

What Recognition Makes Possible

You didn't choose your original money programming. You learned it early, under pressure, before you had any power to question it.

Jennifer's story isn't unique. It's one version of a pattern many people carry for years without seeing clearly.

You're not broken. You're running learned responses that once made sense and no longer serve you. Recognition is where those patterns begin to lose their authority.

Your childhood programming doesn't disappear overnight. It loses its grip the moment you see it clearly.

Chapter 2: Rewriting Your Money Story

"The moment you realize your money story isn't set in stone, everything changes."

Sometimes, a pause is enough to break the script.

Saturday afternoon at Northgate Mall. The weekend crowd flows around Jason as he walks past storefronts, that familiar restless feeling creeping up his chest. He's here for one thing: new running shoes to replace his perfectly fine pair at home.

But that voice in his head whispers the usual script: You've been working so hard. You deserve this.

Outside the electronics store, the new wireless gaming headset gleams in the window—$280. Jason's hand moves instinctively toward his wallet, credit card warm against his fingers.

This loop has controlled him for years, and right now, outside the electronics store, it has found a familiar route. The same analytical brain that plans client presentations is building a polished case for a $280 purchase he didn't come here to make.

Standing there, watching other shoppers stream past, Jason feels that edge between wanting and needing blur. He's earned this, right?

His finger hovers over his phone, ready to order it online.

Then he remembers something from a podcast: What if you paused for just sixty seconds before buying anything?

Jason's Sixty-Second Discovery

Jason glances around the mall, feeling slightly foolish, then sets his phone timer. One minute. He leans against the wall next to a potted plant and just... waits.

The first thirty seconds crawl by like hours. His mind churns with justifications. I work overtime every week. My old headphones are terrible. This would help me relax after those brutal client calls.

This is the part most people miss.

The same analytical mind that spends four days comparing savings account interest rates can build a fully convincing case for a $280 purchase in forty seconds. Not because it's irrational—because it's doing exactly what it does everywhere else. Finding patterns, building arguments, solving for relief.

The problem isn't the conclusion it reaches. It's that it started from anxiety rather than intention.

But somewhere around the forty-second mark, something unexpected happens. The urgency starts to fade. He notices his breathing has slowed down. His shoulders drop slightly.

The timer chimes.

Jason looks at the headset again. The want is still there, but softer now. Manageable. Like turning down the volume on a song that was too loud. He takes a photo of it with his phone instead.

"I'm just looking today," Jason says to the approaching salesperson.

Walking away from that purchase, Jason feels something he hasn't experienced in months during a shopping trip: control. Not forced restraint, but a conscious decision he can live with.

Three weeks later, Jason showed his wife, Leah, the credit card statement over breakfast—$480 lower than the month before. He hadn't changed his income or his circumstances. He'd changed the gap between the urge and the action.

How Patterns Get Interrupted

Jason's mall experience shows a different expression of the same underlying loop: Stress triggers the urge to buy something that promises relief, which brings temporary satisfaction but increases financial stress.

Breaking that loop does not require eliminating the trigger or changing your personality. It requires inserting a pause before the pattern completes—long enough for your conscious mind to catch up with the emotional impulse.

That brief pause is what shifts a decision from automatic reaction to conscious choice. The pattern may still be there, but it is no longer the only thing driving the moment.

From Self-Judgment to Curiosity

My phone buzzes against the wood. Overdraft notice. Negative $47.

The embarrassment hits instantly. Chest tightens. The old voice returns: You're being careless. You should know better.

Then something shifts.

This isn't failure.

It's data.

The same analytical skills that solve complex problems at work stall here. Intelligence, praised everywhere else, turns into friction.

I grab a pen and write down the number the way I would document any engineering problem. No shame. Just observation.

Thirty days later, the random overdrafts are gone. Not because I became someone new, but because the same systematic thinking I trusted everywhere else finally arrived here.

The shift is clear: from shame to curiosity.

Where the Pattern Can Be Interrupted

Jason's sixty-second pause and my shift from shame to curiosity both illustrate the same principle: Pattern interruption creates space for conscious choice. Here's a simple five-step process I call the RESET Method.

This RESET process is your real-time interruption system—five steps for catching money patterns before they hijack your decisions.

Here's what the sequence looks like:

Recognize the trigger. You notice the moment the pattern begins to launch: the urge to avoid, over-research, overspend, check repeatedly, or make the discomfort disappear quickly.

Exhale. Before choosing, create a physiological pause. This isn't just breathing; it's the space between trigger and reaction, long enough for your nervous system to settle and your conscious mind to return.

Separate emotion from data. You name what you feel without letting the feeling become the whole truth. Anxiety may be present, but the number, bill, balance, or decision still needs to be seen clearly.

Evaluate with your adult mind. You ask what is actually needed now. The question is not how to feel perfectly calm, but what action fits the facts, your values, and your current capacity.

Take aligned action. You choose deliberately: buy, delay, decline, check, pay, ask, or close the app until the scheduled review. The point is not perfection. The point is that the pattern no longer chooses for you.

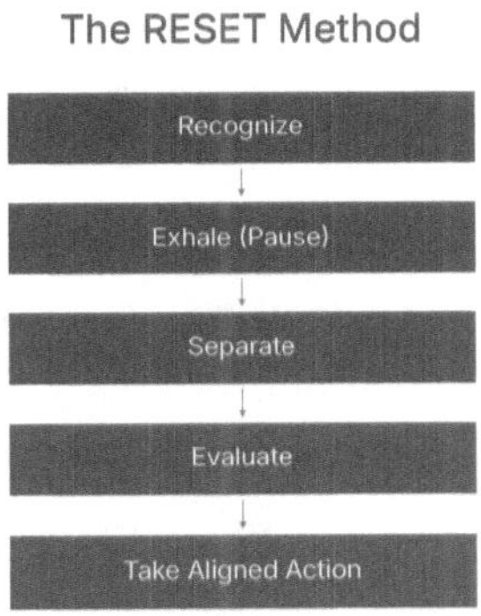

A way to interrupt the pattern without forcing change.

Elena Opens the App

Elena had spent seven years as a project coordinator at a mid-sized architecture firm, a job that required her to track seventeen concurrent dependencies, two contractors who never communicated, and a client who changed his mind every other Tuesday. She was good at complexity. She was good at holding things in her head.

Which made it harder to explain why she hadn't checked her bank balance in three months. An expensive medical bill had arrived in January. Every day of avoidance after that made the imagined number scarier than the real one.

Her breakthrough comes on a quiet Sunday afternoon. She is curled up on the couch with coffee going cold beside her, three months into avoiding the banking app after the medical bill arrived. The anxiety comes before she reaches for the phone: heart racing, breath shallow, shoulders tightening as if the screen is about to deliver a verdict.

This time, she recognizes the pattern before it becomes avoidance. She is not afraid of the app itself. She is afraid of what the unknown number has become during three months of silence. Naming that matters. Once she can see the fear as a pattern, not a command, the next step becomes possible.

Before opening the app, she exhales slowly. Four counts in, six counts out, three times. Her shoulders drop slightly. The fear does not disappear, but it stops occupying the whole room. That pause gives her enough space to separate the emotion from the data.

She asks herself a cleaner question: Is she in immediate financial danger, or is her nervous system treating uncertainty as an emergency? The answer does not make her fearless, but it makes the next action possible. She can open the app for sixty seconds. She can close it afterward. The number can be information instead of punishment.

Her hands still tremble when she taps the screen. The balance appears: $847.22. Not comfortable, but not the $12.50 her imagination had created.

The fear had become larger than the number because the number had been left unseen.

That afternoon, Elena decides to check her balance each morning with coffee. Ten seconds is enough. The pattern has not disappeared, but it no longer has three months of silence to grow inside.

What Changes When the Pattern Breaks

One person started writing their exact balance down every morning. Not to track it. Just to see the number in their own handwriting. The fear of the unknown number had been worse than the number itself. On a phone, the balance can feel like an accusation. In a notebook, it becomes a number.

Another began moving small amounts to savings immediately after checking. Five dollars one day. One dollar the next. The amount wasn't the point. The action was.

Someone else reflected on yesterday's spending while the coffee brewed. Another asked one question before bed: Did I spend money on what mattered today?

None of it was elaborate. None of it needed to be. None of it was a system. All of it was a small act of presence.

Presence is where the pattern first loosens its grip.

What matters here is not affirmation. It is evidence. Most financial affirmations fail because they ask you to say something your nervous system doesn't yet believe. A better starting point is smaller and more honest: If you're interrupting old responses, even briefly, you're already building a different relationship to money—one decision at a time.

When the Response Is No Longer Automatic

Your automatic money patterns aren't permanent features of your personality. They're learned responses that can be interrupted and replaced with conscious choices.

The patterns controlling your financial decisions were installed years ago through repetition and emotional intensity. The RESET process uses the same principles—repetition and positive emotion—to install new patterns that serve your actual goals.

Jason glanced around the mall, feeling slightly foolish, then set his phone timer. One minute. Somewhere around the forty-second mark, the urgency started to fade. In that brief pause, the response was no longer automatic. The impulse was still there, but it wasn't in control. It was the only moment in which his history wasn't running the response.

That sixty-second pause became his gateway to conscious financial choice.

Recognition does not eliminate the pattern.

It changes what the pattern can do.

Interlude: Return

There's a version of this work that becomes another thing to analyze.

You read about the RESET process. You start taking notes. You compare it to other frameworks. You consider whether the five steps are optimally sequenced.

The Loop adapts. It will run inside anything—including this.

Notice if that's happening.

Then continue.

Chapter 3: Your Body's Money Language

Your body decided before you did.

It happens before you read the first number. Before you open the app. Sometimes before your hand even reaches the phone. You have probably been treating that reaction as interference. It isn't. It's information.

Paul was sitting beside his wife at the kitchen table when the old alarm arrived. The spreadsheet was clean. The numbers were stable. Nothing on the screen justified what his body was doing next. His breathing shortened. His shoulders rose. Words left him all at once.

"Are you okay?" Claire asked, noticing his sudden stillness.

Paul blinked, startled by his own reaction. They weren't fighting. There was no crisis. This was just their routine financial check-in, something they'd done dozens of times before.

But his body was responding like they were in the middle of a screaming match about bankruptcy.

That freeze response when money comes up? The tremor when you check your balance? The way your breath catches during financial conversations?

None of this starts with numbers. Your body learned that money conversations meant danger long before it learned what a balance sheet was.

The Old Alarm at the Kitchen Table

Sitting at that kitchen table, watching his wife's concerned face, Paul suddenly understood something. His body's reaction had nothing to do with their current financial situation.

It had everything to do with being eight years old, pressed against the cold floor under his bed while his parents screamed about the electric bill. The floor had shaken with their rage. His small body had soaked up every bit of that money terror.

In that moment, his nervous system learned: Money talk equals danger.

Thirty years later, that alarm still rang. Even during calm budget reviews with his loving wife, his body activated the same protection protocol it had learned decades earlier.

"This isn't about our budget," Paul realized aloud. "This is my eight-year-old nervous system."

For the first time, he could see the pattern clearly enough to interrupt it.

If your body reacted reading that scene, take three slow breaths before continuing.

His adult brain knew their finances were stable, but his nervous system was still running protection software installed three decades earlier.

Over the following weeks, Paul began noticing this pattern everywhere. His breathing would shift when opening bills, even when he knew they had enough money to pay them. His jaw would clench during investment conversations, regardless of how well their portfolio was performing.

But the recognition itself became his superpower. "My body is running an old program," he'd say to himself. "This isn't current reality."

That simple awareness gave him precious seconds of choice between trigger and reaction. Instead of shutting down during money-related discussions, he could pause, breathe, and stay present with his wife.

Six months later, Paul and Claire were reviewing a major financial decision together. During their research conversations, Paul noticed his chest starting to tighten and immediately recognized it as his old pattern activating.

"Give me a second," he said, placing his hand on his chest and taking three slow breaths. "My nervous system thinks this is scary, but I know we're making a smart choice."

Claire smiled. "I love that you can catch that now."

The body signals the pattern before conscious thought arrives.

When Money Feels Like Threat

What Paul experienced at that kitchen table points to something the RESET process alone can't reach. Your body often reacts before your conscious mind has finished interpreting the situation. A money conversation, a low balance, or an unexpected bill can be read not only as information but as threat, especially when earlier life taught your body to associate money with danger. This doesn't mean the body is irrational. It means the body is working from older evidence.

When the body feels safe enough, thinking has more room. Breath steadies, attention widens, and choices become easier to evaluate. When the body shifts into alert, the mind often narrows toward urgency, checking, control, or overanalysis. When the body moves toward shutdown, energy drops and decisions may disappear into avoidance. This body-state framing draws from research on emotional memory and autonomic regulation, but the practical point is simple: Financial clarity improves when the body isn't treating every money signal as an emergency.[1]

If you notice tension rising, even a small interruption can help shift the state—standing up, taking a short walk, or naming the next smallest step.

Most people move between alert and shutdown around money without realizing it. The work is not to force calm. It is to recognize the state early enough to interrupt it. If structural constraints are present—real limits on income or resources—body awareness helps you stay resourced while you work through the practical challenges.

1. Antonio Damasio, Descartes' Error: Emotion, Reason, and the Human Brain (New York: Putnam, 1994).

Thought vs Felt Sensation

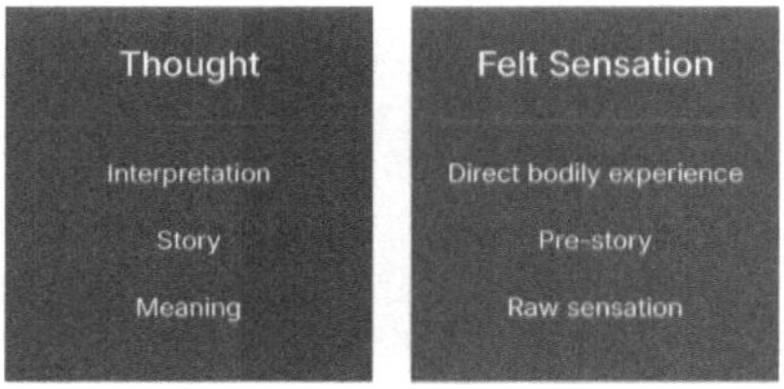

Why clarity often shows up before logic does.

The Forty-Dollar Dress

My own recognition of body-based money programming came through one specific moment that I'll never forget.

By the time we moved to Canada and I earned my P.Eng., our financial situation had transformed. As a structural engineer earning good income, I could afford things. But the $40 dress shame persisted—body memory outlasting circumstances.

Standing in that department store, I felt physically sick. Over $40. When we had enough. When my career was stable. When the numbers said we were fine.

That's when it hit me. My bank account had completely changed. My professional credentials had changed. But my nervous system was still running software from childhood, when every purchase carried survival weight. The old programming was executing through my body memory, not my current reality.

The voice from my childhood whispered: You don't deserve to spend money. Not yet.

My hand stopped on the fabric. I could feel the refusal in my body before I could explain it—chest tight, jaw set, shoulders held too high for a department store on an ordinary day. Nothing about the moment was urgent. That was what made it so revealing. The price was clear. The need was clear. But my body was still reacting as if this small purchase had the weight of consequence it once carried. The hesitation did not belong to the dress. It belonged to an older life.

I stood there for several minutes, long enough that a saleswoman passed twice without approaching, reading something in my posture that said I wasn't ready.

My daughter had already moved on to another rack. My wife was holding up a blouse nearby, checking the seam. Neither of them knew what was happening to me. Nothing visible was happening at all. A man standing in a Canadian department store, holding a dress. Ordinary from the outside. Internally, I was still answering to an older rule: that spending money on anything non-essential carried a moral weight it no longer deserved.

I knew that pattern existed. I had already named it. What I hadn't understood yet was that naming a pattern and interrupting it were not the same skill.

What shifted the moment wasn't a better argument. My daughter came back.

She was still young enough to say exactly what she meant. She held up the dress—blue cotton, simple, nothing elaborate—and asked, "It's nice, Dad. Do you think Mom will like it?"

Something about that question returned me to the actual room. Not to the past, not to the old logic, not to the inherited fear that had attached itself to spending. Just the room: my daughter's face, my wife nearby, the fabric in my hand, the fact that this was a forty-dollar decision and not a referendum on survival.

I bought the dress.

As we walked out of the store, I noticed the change first in my body. The tightness in my chest had eased. My jaw had unclenched. What I felt wasn't triumph or even relief in the dramatic sense. It was the absence of a posture I hadn't realized I had been holding. Some part of me had been prepared for consequence, and the consequence hadn't arrived. The purchase was done. Nothing had fallen apart.

That mattered because it gave my nervous system something it had never really received before: evidence. Not a theory, not a reassurance, not a better explanation. Evidence that spending money, within reasonable limits, didn't automatically produce the danger the old pattern still expected.

I don't want to make the moment sound cleaner than it was. The following week, I stood in a hardware store for twenty minutes unable to buy something I actually needed. The dress hadn't cured anything. What it had done was leave behind one piece of usable evidence. One instance in which the old prediction had failed.

That is how body programming changes. Not through insight alone, but through repeated contradiction. You accumulate experiences that don't match what the nervous system has been expecting, and over time the expectation becomes less automatic.

The $40 dress wasn't a turning point in any dramatic sense. It was a small piece of evidence. But change is often built that way: not from one decisive moment, but from enough moments that the old pattern can no longer claim to be the only truth.

I grew up in a rural part of the Philippines, where my family struggled to make ends meet and every purchase had to be weighed carefully. Spending money, even on necessities, could carry guilt because the next need was never abstract. It might arrive tomorrow, and there might not be enough. That scarcity was real then. The problem was that my body was still treating it as real now.

Standing in that store, I wasn't reacting only to a dress. I was reacting to an older rule: Do not spend unless survival requires it. Buying the dress didn't erase that rule, but it contradicted it. My wife liked the dress, it was within our means, and nothing fell apart. The shame response was not truth about the present. It was data from the past.

That was the real shift. My nervous system had been protecting me from dangers that no longer existed. I had learned to think clearly under pressure in other areas of life, but here, something older was still running. The dress didn't cure the pattern. It gave my body one piece of evidence that the old prediction was no longer always true.

Catching the Signal Early

Elena discovered that her body held the key to deeper change.

During her first weeks of practice, Elena noticed something frustrating. Even when she tried to use the RESET process, her body was already activated—heart pounding, breath shallow—before she could think clearly.

"By the time I realize I'm triggered, my body has already taken over," she told me. "It's like trying to steer a car that's already crashed."

Elena began focusing on the earlier signals. Instead of waiting for full-blown panic, she started noticing the first whispers of activation: a slight tightening in her chest, a subtle shift in her breathing, tension creeping into her shoulders.

The breakthrough came during a conversation with her sister about splitting costs for their mother's care. Normally, this topic sent Elena into immediate shutdown—too overwhelming to even think about.

But this time, she caught the activation early. "I felt my chest start to close," Elena recalls. "And instead of pushing through or running away, I just put my hand on my heart and breathed."

Her sister noticed the pause. "Are you okay?"

"I'm good," Elena said. "Just giving my nervous system a moment to catch up with reality."

The body creates emotional signals tied to past experience—and when those signals go quiet, decisions stall. Not from lack of information, but from the absence of the body's input. Elena could analyze the conversation with her sister logically. What she couldn't do, until she learned to listen to her body, was move through it.

That simple intervention—catching the body's early warning signs and responding with awareness—transformed a conversation that had always ended in tears or avoidance into a productive planning session.

"I didn't change my personality," Elena reflects. "I just learned to recognize when my body was running old protection programs and gave myself permission to choose differently."

When Calm Returns

Understanding your patterns is the first step. Now you can work with your body's natural capacity to settle instead of fighting against outdated programming. This isn't about fixing what's broken. You're not broken. You're learning to access states your body already knows.

When you notice your body shifting into alert or shutdown around money, you have a choice. You can recognize the state, acknowledge what your nervous system is trying to protect you from, and gently guide yourself back toward steadiness.

Some people find it helpful to create a simple physical anchor—a gesture that becomes associated with calm over time. This might be placing a hand on your heart, touching thumb to pinky finger, or taking three intentional breaths. The specific gesture matters less than using it consistently when you're already settled, so your nervous system begins to associate that physical cue with steadiness.

This isn't a conditioning program you need to master. It's simply working with how your body naturally learns through repetition. When you consistently pair a physical gesture with a regulated state, your nervous system learns the association—similar to how athletes use pre-performance routines to access optimal states.

The timeline for this varies, but the key is gentle consistency rather than forced practice. You're not installing new programming overnight. You're helping your body remember that it can settle around money—something it already knows how to do.

What the Body Reveals

You've seen how body awareness works through Paul's budget freeze, my $40 dress moment, and Elena's early-signal breakthrough. These aren't isolated successes—they reveal what becomes visible when people begin noticing their body's money language.

Some people discover the power of catching physical signals early. Like Paul, who learned to notice his chest tightening before full shutdown occurred. That early recognition created space for choice.

Simple physical gestures can make the shift easier. Maria would place her hand on her heart before checking her balance, using that contact to remind her nervous system that looking at numbers was safe.

Some notice that their body responds differently to different money activities. Edward realized his shoulders tensed when opening bills but his breathing stayed calm when planning purchases. That awareness helped him identify which situations needed extra nervous system support.

These examples show what begins to emerge when people pay closer attention to the body's signals. Later chapters will build on this awareness in more practical ways. For now, the important shift is simpler: money behavior becomes easier to understand when the body is no longer left out of the conversation.

Before It Had a Name

Money anxiety is not always a response to the numbers in front of us. Sometimes it begins earlier—in the body, before conscious thought has time to explain what is happening. That is why an old money fear can return even when the present account balance says something different.

Paul discovered this during that budget review with his wife. His chest tightened and his breathing shifted—the same response he had felt watching his parents fight about bills thirty years earlier. That recognition allowed him to pause, breathe, and stay present instead of shutting down.

The forty-dollar dress showed me how deeply those old instructions can remain. Standing in that store—fluorescent lights harsh on the soft cotton fabric—feeling shame over a purchase we could easily afford, I realized my body was still following rules written in a completely different financial reality.

The body learned those instructions under conditions that no longer exist. The work is not to silence them. It is to stop mistaking them for current information.

Chapter 4: When Belief Feels Like Fact

Standing in a Toronto bank lobby, I understood for the first time that I had already stepped back.

My body was there. I could hear the advisor explaining portfolio options. Other clients were nodding, asking questions about asset allocation and rebalancing. I had the money. I had the credentials. I had, by that point, earned my P.Eng. in Ontario after rebuilding a career that had crossed multiple countries.

The thought running in my head was simple: They probably learned this from their parents.

I left without asking about the investment account.

Not because I lacked the money. Because some part of me still believed that serious money planning was for people who had started differently than I had.

That belief didn't feel like a belief. It felt like an accurate reading of the room.

That is the thing about a limiting belief. It presents as perception.

Clara's version looked different. The logic was the same.

She stared at a savings challenge post on her phone: "Save $5 a day for 30 days." Her immediate thought came fast: I can barely cover rent. This isn't for me.

She scrolled past, but that familiar weight settled in her chest again. The feeling wasn't just discouragement. It was recognition. The old category returning: people like us.

This time, she caught it before it settled.

She paused, placed her hand on her heart, and took three slow breaths.

"Wait," she said aloud to her empty apartment. "What if this is exactly for someone like me?"

The shift began there.

Not because her financial situation changed. Because the sentence in her head stopped sounding like fact.

Clara's Breakthrough

Over the next week, Clara tracked her automatic money thoughts like a scientist observing patterns. She noticed the same limiting beliefs recurring across different situations.

Each thought felt like absolute truth, but Clara began to recognize them as programs running in her mind: software installed years ago that she'd never consciously chosen.

The breakthrough came during a conversation with her coworker about retirement savings.

"I should probably start a retirement account," her coworker mentioned casually.

Clara's instant internal response: People like us don't plan that far ahead. We just survive paycheck to paycheck.

But this time, Clara caught the thought. She realized she'd grouped herself and her coworker into the same limiting category automatically, despite the fact that her coworker was actively talking about long-term planning.

"What if I'm not stuck in survival mode?" Clara wondered. "What if I just learned to think I was?"

Clara began experimenting with different thoughts: What if I can plan for my future? What if small amounts do add up? What if I'm more capable than I realized?

The shift wasn't immediate or dramatic. Some days, the old voice still dominated. But Clara noticed that when she consciously chose different thoughts, her actions began to change too.

Within two weeks, Clara had opened her first savings account in five years. Not because her financial situation had changed, but because she'd started questioning the voice that told her savings "weren't for people like her."

Six months later, Clara had $500 in savings and a different relationship with the voice that had been making her financial decisions. She still heard it. She just no longer assumed it was telling the truth.

"I realized I'd been letting a voice from my childhood run my adult financial decisions," Clara reflected. "Once I could hear it clearly, I could choose whether to listen to it or not."

The Voice Loses Its Authority

Building on Clara's breakthrough and my own recognition process, truth-testing reveals how limiting beliefs operate at the thought level. Where body awareness catches the Smart Struggle Loop in your nervous system, truth-testing catches it in your mind.

Work in cognitive psychology, especially Aaron Beck's, helped establish that examining and reframing thoughts can alter the way later decisions are processed. When you consciously question a belief and practice an alternative, you're not just changing your mind—you're changing the way your brain handles future decisions.[1]

Body awareness reveals the automatic responses of the body. Truth-testing reveals the automatic responses of the mind—the beliefs driving decisions after your nervous system settles.

Who Is Speaking?

When you're about to make a financial decision, whose voice do you hear?

Sometimes it sounds like a harsh instructor: You should know better by now. Everyone else has figured this out already. Sometimes it sounds like an absent parent: Figure it out yourself. No one is coming to save you. Sometimes it sounds like a paranoid analyst, scanning for catastrophe in every choice, or an eternal pessimist, assuming good outcomes are for other people.

At other times, the voice is quieter but just as powerful. It may sound like a shameful accountant whispering, Look at this mess. A responsible person wouldn't be in this situation. Or a helpless child insisting, This is too complicated. I just can't do this.

These voices feel personal, but they are usually expressions of deeper money beliefs. Beneath those behavioral patterns, most people's beliefs tend to fall into one of three deeper patterns:

---

1. Aaron T. Beck, Cognitive Therapy and the Emotional Disorders (New York: Penguin, 1979).

Survival mode says you're only trying to get by, so planning for growth feels unrealistic.

Skepticism says wealth belongs to people with luck, privilege, or knowledge you don't have.

Perfectionism says you must understand everything before you can act safely.

Once you can hear the voice clearly and name the pattern beneath it, you stop mistaking it for truth.

The Spreadsheet Couldn't Decide

Michael lived inside spreadsheets. Before buying anything over fifty dollars, he'd create comparison tables with weighted scoring systems. His wife Marie called it "analysis paralysis." Michael called it "being responsible."

The breakthrough came during a conversation about their first rental property investment. After eight months of research, they finally recognized the pattern: perfectionism masking fear.

"When will you have enough information?" Marie asked, not angry—just genuinely curious.

Michael opened his mouth to explain why more data meant better decisions, but the words stopped. He recognized that familiar sensation in his chest—the tightness that came whenever he had to choose without perfect certainty.

"I'm not being thorough," Michael realized aloud. "I'm being scared."

Michael began to notice the belief running his decisions: "If I don't analyze every possibility perfectly, I'll make a catastrophic mistake."

He sat with that thought. Where had it come from? His father—brilliant engineer, terrible with money—had lost their house in a bad investment Michael barely recalled. But he'd heard about it his entire childhood. The lesson learned: One wrong choice destroys everything.

Then, Michael looked at his own life for contradictory evidence. Was that belief true? He thought about his career decisions, his marriage, relocating cities. He'd made dozens of major choices without perfect information. Not one had been catastrophic. Some worked better than others, but he'd adjusted and moved forward each time.

A different story began to emerge: "Good enough information plus action beats perfect information that never moves."

Three days later, instead of opening another spreadsheet to model additional scenarios, Michael signed the pre-approval paperwork. His hands shook slightly, but he signed anyway.

Six months later, the rental property was generating steady income. Michael hadn't become fearless. He had become someone who could sign paperwork while his hands were still shaking—and trust that the decision didn't need to be perfect to be right.

"I used to think confidence came from knowing everything," he reflected. "Now I know it comes from trusting myself to handle whatever happens after I choose."

What would happen if you tested that belief against your actual life evidence?

What No Longer Feels True

When you catch a limiting belief, you start to see it as code running in your mental system. "I can't save" is code. "Debt is normal" is code. "Investing is too risky" is code. Most of this code was installed when you were too young to choose it consciously.

People often notice their own life contains evidence that contradicts the belief. This isn't about positive affirmations that feel fake—it's about examining whether your belief matches your real experience.

If you're operating from survival mode, when have you taken a calculated risk that worked out? When have you recovered from a financial setback?

If you're operating from skepticism, what financial skills have you learned that you didn't grow up knowing? When have you successfully learned something complex in another area of life?

If you're operating from perfectionism, when have you taken imperfect action and learned through doing?

The power of this recognition comes from using your own life as proof. Your brain can dismiss general success stories, but it struggles to argue with your personal experience.

When old programming activates, you have a brief window before it hijacks your decisions. That's your opportunity to catch the belief and choose differently.

The First Extra Payment

Elena's story shows what this recognition looks like in practice. For three years, Elena had been telling herself she would get serious about her debt "when I understand it better." She'd bookmarked articles about debt payoff strategies, downloaded budgeting and debt tracker apps, and read personal finance content about getting out of debt.

But every time she got close to making an extra payment, her mind would flood with cautionary thoughts: What if I need that money for something else? What if another bill comes up? I should probably get a clearer picture before I commit any extra funds.

Elena began to catch the belief: "I need to understand everything perfectly before I can tackle my debt." She recognized this as her perfectionist pattern.

Then, she examined her own life for contradictory evidence. She'd learned to drive without perfect knowledge of automotive engineering. She'd moved to a new city without knowing every street. She'd taken her current job without understanding the company perfectly.

A new story began to take shape: "I can start with small amounts while I learn, and imperfect action beats perfect inaction."

Elena made her first extra payment—$50 directly to her highest-rate credit card. Not because she'd mastered debt elimination, but because she'd recognized her perfectionist belief as outdated programming.

Over the next year, Elena continued making small additional payments monthly while learning more about her full debt picture. Her highest-rate balance dropped by more than $800 but, more importantly, she'd transformed from someone paralyzed by the need for perfect knowledge into someone who learns by doing.

Elena's transformation shows that belief change isn't about becoming fearless—it's about acting despite fear with beliefs that support growth rather than paralysis. What small action could prove your new belief to yourself?

The Belief Beneath the Decision

An untested belief can guide a money decision before you realize it is there. It does not announce itself as an assumption. It arrives as caution, intelligence, responsibility, or common sense.

That is what changed for Michael. The problem was not that he needed one more spreadsheet. It was the belief beneath the spreadsheet: perfect information would keep catastrophe away. Once he saw that belief clearly, he could look at his own history differently. He had already made imperfect decisions that turned out well enough. He had already survived uncertainty. The decision did not become risk-free. It became possible.

A belief that goes unexamined does not feel like a choice. It feels like a fact. Examining it is what returns the choice to you.

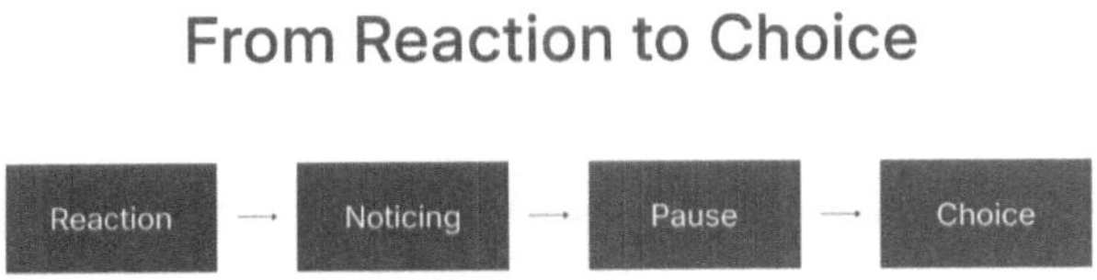

How awareness creates choice.

Chapter 5: The Authority to Decide

The Invoice I Kept Reopening

The invoice took me two days to send.

The work had been completed, the extra hours were documented, and the extra amount was fair. I had tracked the time carefully because that is what I do. As an engineer, I trust records, scope, and evidence. Still, the number sat there while I kept reopening the draft and asking a question the facts had already answered.

The amount was $1,200. I had spent forty-seven hours doing the work and two days deciding whether I deserved to be paid for it.

That was the moment the pattern became visible in a new form. The Smart Struggle Loop wasn't showing up as research this time. It was showing up as hesitation, shame, and the quiet belief that asking to be paid fairly was somehow asking too much.

That night, looking at the sent invoice, I understood the problem differently.

I wasn't failing at money because I lacked intelligence or effort. I was failing to lead it.

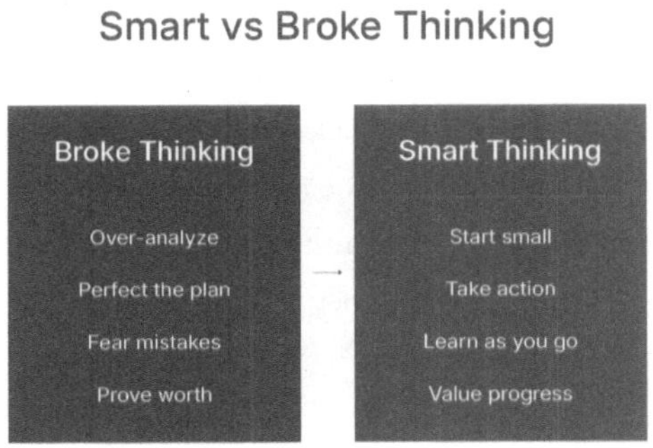

Why being "smart" isn't the advantage you think it is.

The better question was no longer, "Why is money so hard?" It was, "Who is actually directing this part of my life?"

Pleading With Money

This is not where the book asks you to work harder. It is where the work becomes lighter.

Recognition shows you the Loop. Leadership gives that recognition somewhere to go. The point is not to add another layer of pressure to your money life. The point is to build enough internal authority that every decision no longer has to be fought from scratch.

You can recognize the Smart Struggle Loop. You can catch your nervous system activating. You can identify the limiting belief.

But knowing isn't the same as leading.

Someone operating as money's employee checks accounts obsessively, panics at unexpected bills, and lets financial anxiety dictate the emotional tone of the day. Someone operating with authority reviews the same information, sees the pattern, adjusts the system, and does not hand the entire day over to the account balance.

The RESET process gives you pattern interruption tools. Body awareness helps you notice when your nervous system is treating money as threat. Truth-testing helps you examine the belief behind the reaction. But beliefs change behavior only so far. At some point, the deeper question becomes identity.

Who are you being when money gets difficult?

For years, I had been treating myself like an awkward guest in my own money life — like I was visiting someone else's money instead of directing my own. I followed whatever money advice I found, hoping for permission to spend. I reacted to whatever happened in my accounts. I waited for my salary to give me permission to feel safe. I asked my spreadsheet for permission to buy something I wanted.

But that night, something shifted.

The next morning, nothing looked dramatic on paper. The account hadn't become generous overnight. The uncertainty hadn't disappeared. What changed was smaller and more important: I checked once, wrote down what needed to happen, and stopped re-opening the problem as if more looking could change it.

It was the first time I handled my money like something I was responsible for directing, not something I was pleading with to calm me down.

I realized I had been waiting for someone else to lead my money life when I was the only one qualified for the job.

The change did not happen overnight. But it began with a simple decision: I was going to stop following in my own money life and start leading. This engineering mindset felt natural once I saw it clearly. I had spent years treating technical problems as systems that could be understood, designed, and improved. I had finally applied the same approach to money — not as a motivational slogan, but as a responsibility.

What Authority Looks Like

If the language of "leading" your money feels unfamiliar, that is understandable. Many people have been passive around money for so long that authority feels almost unnatural at first. But authority does not mean control over every outcome. It means you stop handing over your choices to fear, shame, habit, or account-balance panic.

Behavior that feels personally meaningful and internally chosen tends to sustain with less maintenance than behavior driven only by external pressure. When a behavior becomes connected to who you believe yourself to be, it no longer depends entirely on mood, fear, or reward. You are not forcing yourself to perform the behavior from the outside. You are acting in a way that feels increasingly consistent with the person you are becoming.

That is how the earlier tools begin to work together. RESET helps you catch the automatic response. Body awareness helps you stay regulated enough to respond. Truth-testing helps you examine the belief driving the reaction. Identity gives all of that work a place to live.

The point is not that you never react. The point is that the reaction no longer has final authority.

When you face a money decision, the old response may still appear: "I can't afford this," "I shouldn't spend money," "Something bad will happen," "I need more information first." RESET helps you catch it before it takes over. Body awareness helps calm the urgency or shame underneath it. Truth-testing helps you examine whether the belief is actually true.

Then authority asks the larger question:

Who is deciding now?

The difference plays out in everyday moments. Someone operating from an employee identity checks a bank balance and thinks, "Only $800 left. I need to be careful." Someone operating with authority sees the same $800 and thinks, "I have $800 in my operating account, $200 going to savings Friday, and I'm on track with my quarterly plan." When an unexpected car repair costs $400, the old identity feels victimized: "Why does this always happen to me?" Authority problem-solves: "I'll use $400 from the emergency fund, then rebuild it over the next two months with the system I already have."

This is close to what psychologists describe as moving from an external to an internal locus of control — the difference between feeling controlled by circumstances and seeing yourself as someone who can respond within them. The circumstances may still be real. The bill may still be real. The uncertainty may still be real. But the authority to respond returns to you.

The Parking Lot Decision

Maria sat in her parked car outside the small business development center, hands gripping the steering wheel so hard her knuckles went white. For eighteen months, she had carried a business plan for her translation services. She had researched rates, identified target clients, and even built a simple website mockup. But every time she thought about actually launching, her chest tightened and the familiar voice returned:

"Who are you to call yourself a business owner? You're just someone who speaks two languages."

That afternoon was supposed to be different. She had come to register her business name — the one concrete step that would make the business real. But sitting there in the parking lot, she couldn't move. Her phone showed 3:47 p.m. The office closed at four.

Then Maria used the tools she had been practicing. RESET helped her catch the freezing pattern before it became another delay. Body awareness helped her notice how risk showed up in her body. Truth-testing had already helped her challenge the belief that "real business owners" were fundamentally different from her. But this moment required something more — not just using the tools one by one, but letting them point toward a decision.

She caught the pattern. She regulated her racing heart with three deep breaths. She reminded herself of the evidence: she solved valuable translation problems every day. She had already done the work. She had already prepared. Now she had to choose.

Would she operate as someone waiting for permission? Or as the person responsible for directing her own business?

Maria placed her hand on her chest, felt her racing heart, and made a decision.

"I'm not someone trying to start a business," she said quietly. "I'm someone who runs one."

The shift was not pure confidence — it was steadier than that. More like permission she could grant herself. The business owner identity was not something she would become eventually. It was something she could choose now. She grabbed her folder and walked into the office with two minutes to spare.

"Business name registration," she told the clerk, her voice steadier than she expected.

The Name She Registered

Three months later, Maria had landed her first corporate client at $95 per hour, three times what she had earned in her previous job. But the real change was not only the income. It was how she introduced herself. "I run a translation business" replaced "I'm trying to start something." That shift changed how she priced her services, how she negotiated with clients, and how she made money decisions.

"I used to think I'd feel like a business owner once I was successful," Maria reflected. "Then I realized it worked the other way. I had to stop waiting for success to give me permission."

Maria did not wait until circumstances proved she was capable. She used RESET to catch her hesitation pattern, body awareness when her chest tightened, and truth-testing to challenge the belief that "real business owners" were different from her. But the decision was larger than any single tool. She stopped asking the world to confirm an identity she had not yet claimed.

That is what authority does. It does not make the uncertainty disappear. It does not guarantee the outcome. It does not remove the need for systems, evidence, planning, or skill. It changes who is allowed to decide.

Maria's story began in a parking lot, but the same question appears in ordinary money decisions every day. Am I someone who waits for the account balance to tell me whether I'm safe? Am I someone who waits for perfect information before acting? Am I someone who needs permission to charge fairly, save consistently, spend without shame, or build something larger? Or am I the person responsible for directing this part of my life?

That is the authority Chapter 5 is about. Not control over every outcome. Not confidence all the time. Not pretending money is simple.

The authority to decide.

What Keeps Repeating

In Chapter 1, you identified your behavioral money pattern—the automatic response your nervous system runs when money comes up: avoidance, hoarding, overgiving, denial, or perfectionism. Those patterns describe what you do when a financial trigger arrives.

This section works at a different level: not what you do around money, but who you believe you are in relation to it. The same behavioral avoidance can run inside an earner identity, a protector identity, or a deferrer identity. The behavioral pattern is the symptom. The identity assumption is the operating system beneath it.

Most people operate from one of three limiting identities around money. Recognizing your current identity is the first step in shifting to leadership.

Some people operate as earners—believing their worth comes from how much they make. They work constantly but struggle with spending decisions. They chase money instead of leading it.

Others operate as protectors—believing safety comes from saving every penny. They save but rarely invest or spend strategically. Every dollar spent feels like personal failure.

Others operate as deferrers—believing money is too complicated or overwhelming to engage with directly. They handle basics competently but step back from the deeper decisions that would serve their long-term goals.

These identities play out in specific ways. The earner works overtime constantly but freezes when deciding how to actually use earned money—productivity is high, but strategy is reactive. The protector might sit on $20,000 in a savings account earning 0.5% interest while avoiding investment opportunities that feel "too risky." The deferrer handles basics competently but claims "I'm just not a money person" when facing decisions that would serve long-term goals.

Which identity resonates most strongly? Notice what happens in your body as you read each description. That physical response reveals which identity runs most powerfully in your system.

If recognizing yourself in one of these identities feels uncomfortable, that awareness is the first step toward transformation. You're not broken—you're operating from a limiting identity that can be upgraded.

This is the Smart Struggle Loop at the identity layer—where your automatic responses begin to change without effort.

The Role You Kept Playing

The shift does not always announce itself. It appears in small decisions that only seem significant in retrospect.

That same invoice became one of those decisions. The additional work was real. I had the documentation. The charge was fair. For two days, the old voice tried to turn fairness into trouble: Don't make waves. They might not hire you again. Just absorb it. That's what professionals do.

What was different this time was that I could see the voice as separate from me. It was not judgment. It was an old pattern trying to keep me small enough to avoid conflict or rejection. The question became simpler than the pattern wanted it to be: Was the additional work documented, and was the charge fair? The answer to both was yes.

I sent the invoice. The client paid without question. What settled in me afterward was not triumph, but something quieter: the realization that I was allowed to be paid for work I had actually done.

The older version of me would have absorbed the cost and called it professionalism. What I understood more clearly now was that absorbing real, documented work without charge was not professionalism. It was self-erasure wearing the language of virtue.

The same shift showed up later in a different form. About six months into using an automated money system, I realized I was still checking my operating account twice a day. The automation was working. Nothing required my attention. But I was checking anyway — a reflex, a form of anxious surveillance that had learned to present itself as responsibility.

The question that finally exposed the habit was simple: what exactly was I looking for? I did not have a good answer. I was not looking for a specific problem or a specific number. I was repeating the act of monitoring because monitoring felt like control.

For two weeks, I limited myself to one weekly check: Sunday evening, same time, same purpose — confirm that the automation had run, note any anomaly, close the app. That was all.

What I discovered was that the daily checking had not been creating control. It had been creating anxiety. Each time I checked and saw a number that was neither disastrous nor fully comfortable, my nervous system treated it as something unresolved. By checking less, I stopped generating that loop. The accounts moved exactly as designed. Nothing collapsed. The weekly check was enough, and because it happened on a schedule, it was easier to approach with clarity than with the low-grade dread that had accompanied the unscheduled checks.

That was what the identity shift looked like in practice: not a dramatic declaration, but a scheduled Sunday evening, a single review, and a closed app.

It appeared again with a professional tool I used regularly in my work. It cost a few hundred dollars each year. Every time renewal came around, I would spend two or three days reconsidering it — researching alternatives, building a case for why I might not need it, nearly cancelling it, and then renewing it at the last moment while feeling guilty about the expense.

The pattern was not really about the money. The tool was worth the cost. The pattern was the internal permission structure I was still running: the belief that spending money on something useful for my own work required extended justification, as though the default answer should always be no.

The shift was not about the subscription itself. It was about recognizing that the justification loop was the real problem. When renewal came around the following year, I renewed it in a few minutes, filed the receipt, and moved on. No research. No alternatives. No guilt.

The time I had spent in previous years constructing a case for a renewal I was always going to make had a cost. So did the anxiety. Neither appeared on the receipt, but both were real.

This is what authority begins to change: not only the major decisions, but the smaller negotiations that quietly drain attention, time, and confidence. The invoice goes out. The account stays closed until the scheduled review. The renewal happens. Each decision is small, but each one removes a loop that was never necessary.

That is the role you stop playing: not the person who waits for money to grant permission, and not the person who confuses anxious checking with responsibility.

The person who decides.

Interlude: The Night It Returned

It was after midnight, long after I thought this part of my life was supposed to feel settled.

The systems were working. Bills were handled. The emergency fund existed. On paper, there was nothing urgent to solve.

Still, I was awake.

I refreshed the account again. Then again. A small market drop, nothing dramatic, and the old pressure was back before I could name it. Not panic exactly. Something quieter. More familiar than that. The feeling that if I just thought hard enough, checked carefully enough, watched closely enough, I could prevent uncertainty from becoming loss.

I knew the pattern. That did not stop it from running.

That was the part I hadn't expected. I had assumed recognition would feel more victorious than this. Cleaner. More final.

Instead, it felt human.

By morning, nothing had changed except the exhaustion. The numbers were the same. The uncertainty was still there. So was I.

Some patterns don't disappear when you understand them. They just lose the right to call themselves truth.

PART TWO: EARNING

Recognition isn't enough.

Now the work turns practical: how value becomes visible, usable, and repeatable.

Chapter 6: What You Already Know

The hardest skills to price are usually the ones that have become automatic.

When I arrived in Ontario in 2003, my resume listed eleven years of international structural engineering work across multiple countries. Projects. Certifications. What it didn't list—because I didn't know how to say it—was what I could actually do that other engineers couldn't.

I had coordinated across language barriers on active construction sites in Saudi Arabia, where a small misunderstanding could create real consequences. I had worked on projects in Singapore where information was incomplete, decisions were urgent, and trust had to be earned faster because I wasn't local. I had made teams in countries I hadn't grown up in trust drawings they hadn't drawn. Each move had reset me to some version of beginner, even when the work itself wasn't new.

None of that appeared on my resume. I called myself a structural engineer.

That gap—between what I could deliver and what I could bring myself to claim—cost me two years of underpricing that no credential could fix.

Maya stared at her credit card statement, minimum payment due in three days. She had ten years of experience managing supply chains, training employees, and fixing broken processes. None of it felt like something you could turn into immediate relief.

That was the mistake. The shift wasn't about learning something new. It was about seeing what she already knew through a different lens.

Even after the identity work in Part One, this is where many people stall. Familiar skill rarely feels valuable from the inside. What you do every day starts to look ordinary to you, even when it solves problems other people find frustrating, expensive, or overwhelming. I know that blindness well; I used to mistake familiarity for smallness.

That is the difference between the employee lens and the leader lens.

Through the employee lens: "I just do basic logistics. Anyone in my role could do this. It's nothing special."

Through the leader lens: "I turn chaos into systems people can actually use. Small businesses struggle with exactly this, and they pay for help."

Same person. Same skills. Different interpretation.

The work you call basic may represent years of pattern recognition, judgment, and problem-solving that your brain has made automatic. Automation makes a skill feel ordinary. It does not make it unimportant. What you do with ease may be exactly what someone else can't do without help.

What changes here is not your skill set. It is your interpretation of it. Work that feels small from the inside can look very different from the outside—especially to someone who needs that problem solved.

This is the shift Maya begins to make.

The Skill She Had Stopped Seeing

Maya had been solving the problem for years. She just hadn't recognized it as something other people would pay to have solved.

The shift began when Maya stopped dismissing her coordination skills as ordinary. What she had treated as background work was solving problems other people found difficult.

When a friend mentioned that her catering business was struggling with delivery logistics, Maya recognized the same coordination challenges she handled at work. "I could probably help with that."

She stopped treating daily problem-solving as background noise and started seeing it as expertise. The work she had been doing for years became visible as something other people needed.

"The hardest part wasn't the technical work," she admitted. "It was claiming expertise publicly. But staying invisible hurt more than the fear of being seen."

Maya's shift points to a pattern you may recognize in yourself: The work that feels most ordinary to you is often the work other people experience as difficult, valuable, and worth paying for.

Maya's automatic dismissal mirrors Jennifer's pattern from Chapter 1. Jennifer avoided her numbers because looking felt like proof of failure. Maya dismissed her coordination ability because familiarity made it seem worthless. The details were different, but the structure was the same. Once each of them interrupted that pattern, what had been hidden became usable.

What Familiarity Had Hidden

When you apply the leader lens to your own capabilities, something shifts in what stands out.

Leaders begin to notice outcomes hiding in ordinary work. Not skills, not credentials, not job titles—concrete results that appear so routinely they've become invisible. The coordination work that prevents chaos. The translation skill that eliminates confusion. The technical explanation that collapses three-week learning curves. What you've automated through repetition, others struggle with desperately.

Leaders notice demand without chasing it. The problems you solve reflexively are the same problems keeping others stuck. What feels basic to you represents exactly what someone else can't figure out. Your "just logistics" is their unsolvable delivery nightmare. Your "simple explanation" is their expensive consultant fee.

Leaders notice evidence where others see "just experience." The difference between "I've been doing this for ten years" and "I consistently produce this specific result" isn't résumé language—it's visibility. Years disappear into vagueness. Outcomes become recognizable value.

Leaders notice specificity where others broadcast generality. "I help businesses" stays invisible to everyone, including the person saying it. "I reduce delivery costs through route optimization" becomes visible to the exact people struggling with delivery costs. The narrower the problem, the clearer the value.

Leaders notice cross-industry patterns. The same problem-solving that works in one context often transfers to completely different industries when properly recognized. Coordination skills don't care about industry boundaries. Systems thinking applies everywhere. Technical translation crosses domains freely.

What changes isn't what you can do. What changes is what you notice about what you've always been doing—and who needs exactly that capability.

Before moving on, take a few minutes to make that recognition concrete.

Write down two simple lists.

First: problems people already bring to you.

Second: what changes after you help.

Don't look for a business idea yet. Look for repeated usefulness. What do people ask you to explain, organize, simplify, fix, translate, check, or make easier? What outcome appears because you were involved?

Maya didn't begin by naming a monetizable skill. She began by noticing that people relied on her to make chaos workable.

Your monetizable skill often begins there: inside the problem other people already trust you to solve.

More Than Technical Skill

Owen's story shows how technical expertise becomes visible. As an IT director, Owen translated complex technical requirements into user-friendly processes. His employee mindset dismissed this: "IT directors are common."

Owen applied the RESET process—the story was "everyone can do this," the fact was "I successfully reduce typical three-week learning curves to five days." The technical translation work he'd been doing for years became visible as valuable capability.

"The value wasn't in the hours—it was in years of experience making those hours effective," Owen reflected.

If your skills feel too niche or too technical, that specialization is exactly what makes capability visible. The more specific the problem you solve, the more recognizable you become to people facing that exact challenge.

The Blind Spot Around Value

Even after the leader-lens shift begins to hold, certain patterns can keep skills invisible.

The generality trap is common. “Business consulting” stays invisible to everyone, including the person saying it. “Inventory reduction for retail stores” becomes visible to the exact people struggling with inventory. The broader the description, the harder it is for anyone — including you — to see the actual value.

The self-doubt discount is another pattern. When truth-testing has not fully taken hold, lingering employee thinking can make you minimize the value of your capability. What you save someone is not determined by how confident you feel. It is determined by the problem you actually solve.

The perfectionism block keeps many people stuck. RESET helps you catch when perfectionism is pretending to be thoroughness. Real-world feedback reveals capability value faster than endless preparation.

Recognizing these patterns matters because invisible value is not usually absent value. It is often value hidden by vague language, old self-doubt, or preparation that never reaches the market.

The Value Already There

The value was not missing. It had become too familiar to notice.

The catering business had a logistics problem. Maya had been solving logistics problems every day for a decade. The only thing that changed was that she stopped calling it something else.

The work from the earlier chapters has a practical use here. You have already practiced catching the voice that dismisses your own capability. Use that same recognition. When you hear "anyone could do this," treat it the way you have learned to treat any other automatic thought — as a pattern, not a verdict.

Your monetizable skill often begins inside the problem other people already trust you to solve.

The shift from invisible to visible does not require new capability. It requires clearer perception.

In practice, that shift often begins the moment you stop treating familiar problem-solving as background noise and start naming the result it creates.

What becomes visible here changes everything that follows. The systems, structures, and practical implementation in the next chapter all work differently once you can finally see the value in what you already know.

Chapter 7: Income You Can Count On

A reliable money system is not a productivity system. Its purpose is to reduce the moments when anxiety, overthinking, and avoidance get a chance to take over.

Most people try to solve unstable income by working harder, taking more projects, answering faster, or staying available to everyone. But effort doesn't create reliability when the underlying pattern remains invisible.

This chapter helps you see where reliability breaks: unexplained success, reinvention fatigue, reactive availability, isolated projects, and activity that looks productive without producing stable results.

Marcus had left a brand strategy role at a mid-size agency because he was tired of building other people's systems. He understood audiences. He understood data. He understood, with the particular confidence of someone who had spent years doing something well, that he could do this on his own.

For three months, the results proved him right. His social media consulting generated $3,800 across twelve engagements. But by January, the pattern beneath the numbers became impossible to ignore—each project felt like starting from scratch, different timelines every time, unpredictable revenue.

Marcus had built a career on recognizing patterns in other people's businesses. He had simply not turned that skill on himself. The feast-or-famine cycle felt like being on a money roller coaster he couldn't control.

If you've experienced this whiplash—celebrating income one month, panicking about bills the next—you already know the problem this chapter solves. Sporadic success proves your skills have value. But unpredictable revenue produces exactly the money anxiety you're working to escape.

By February, Marcus had learned something crucial: having a skill that generates money isn't the same as generating money reliably.

What makes income reliable instead of sporadic? The difference isn't working harder or finding better clients. The difference is understanding why reliability breaks down—and why effort alone can't fix it.

The Income Start-Over Problem

Income doesn't usually feel unstable because people aren't trying hard enough.

It feels unstable because success arrives without explanation. One month works. The next doesn't. There's no clear reason why—just noise. You celebrate when revenue appears, panic when it vanishes, and search desperately for patterns that might predict what happens next.

When outcomes can't be traced back to anything intelligible, effort turns frantic. You work harder, widen your reach, post more frequently, reach out to more contacts. You tell yourself the calm will arrive once you find the right rhythm or reach the right volume.

Marcus discovered the quieter problem when his chaos persisted despite six months of sustained hustle: he had no way to distinguish between the months that worked and the months that didn't. The income didn't feel random because he wasn't trying. It felt random because nothing in how he operated made the difference visible.

Chaos doesn't just come from unpredictable demand. It also comes from treating expertise like a custom art project every single time.

Every engagement feels like inventing a new approach. You start from scratch with each client—different communication style, different deliverable format, different timeline. The work itself might be excellent, but the process of delivering it drains you more with each iteration.

As effort increases, exhaustion often grows faster than revenue. You assume customization demonstrates care and quality. What you're actually doing is burning through cognitive energy on logistics instead of the strategic work that creates real value.

The exhaustion isn't from doing too much work. It's from deciding how to do the same work differently every single time. When Marcus looked at his fourth month of delivery chaos, he realized he had solved his client's problem brilliantly and then spent three days reinventing how to document and hand it off. The expertise was sound. The delivery machinery didn't exist yet.

Client relationships can also feel draining in ways that don't seem to connect to revenue stability—until you notice the pattern.

You respond to some emails immediately and others take days. You're available for calls whenever clients need you, then resentful about the interruptions. You assume responsiveness means immediate availability. What actually happens is that the irregularity produces anxiety for everyone involved.

The more effort you invest, the more tension grows for both you and your clients. They never quite know when to expect responses. You never quite know when you'll get uninterrupted time for deep work. The relationship feels reactive—like you're constantly putting out fires rather than serving clients strategically.

What clients actually need isn't faster responses. They need a rhythm they can plan around. A client who knows you respond on Tuesday and Thursday mornings feels more served than a client who gets an immediate reply at 11 p.m. on a Sunday but nothing for three days after. One produces predictability. The other produces the question: when is it coming?

Revenue can also feel unstable because each project feels like the last relationship you'll ever have with that client.

You complete excellent work. The client is satisfied. Then the relationship just... ends. You start hunting for the next client from scratch, beginning the whole cycle again. Project completion feels like relationship conclusion.

The work expands, yet you still find yourself starting over. You assume successful project delivery should naturally lead to ongoing work, yet somehow it rarely does. What's actually happening is that without explicit ongoing connection, momentum dies the moment you deliver final results.

Marcus counted four clients who went silent after excellent work—not because they were dissatisfied, but because the project had a clear end date and he never raised what would happen on the other side of it. The ending was structural, not relational.

Finally, improvement can feel impossible when you can't distinguish between activity and effectiveness.

You're working constantly. You're trying new approaches, reaching out to prospects, creating content, networking. Some months generate revenue. Others don't. You can't identify what actually makes the difference, so you keep doing everything and hoping something sticks.

Despite all that effort, clarity never arrives. You mistake all the motion for progress. What's actually missing is any way to see which activities produce results and which just fill time. Without that visibility, you're solving a mystery by working harder at everything simultaneously.

The work diary Marcus kept for thirty days was the most uncomfortable thing he'd done during the review. Not because it revealed inadequacy—it revealed the opposite. Two activities generated nearly all his revenue. He'd been spending 70 percent of his time on the other eight. He hadn't been failing at effort. He'd been very effectively optimizing the wrong things.

The Model Beneath the Work

The thought sounded principled, but it was panic protecting chaos. What Marcus called quality was often exhaustion in disguise. He had confused constant reinvention with care.

His capability was never the issue. His delivery model was. He was working like a skilled contractor inside a system that needed to function like a business. Once he saw that, reliability stopped feeling generic and started feeling like proof that his work could hold.

Marcus is still working on it. Some months are steadier than others. The feast-or-famine pattern has quieted, but it hasn't disappeared completely. What changed first wasn't the revenue. It was that he stopped pretending the chaos would fix itself if he just worked harder.

When the Work Holds

When I started helping local contractors improve their project coordination, my first few engagements were successful but exhausting. By the fifth engagement, the pattern had become impossible to ignore.

I had solved the same coordination problem four times. I had different notes for each one. Each time, I had treated the work as if it were new.

I had been an engineer for twenty years. I didn't solve structural problems by inventing a new method each time. I applied tested approaches to specific conditions. I documented what worked. I built on what had been learned. I had simply never extended that logic to the work I did for myself.

The recognition was uncomfortable in the way useful recognitions tend to be: it was so obvious, once I could see it, that I had to ask how I had missed it for so long.

That question followed me into the next engagement.

Invented from Scratch

Nathan experienced the same pattern as an IT consultant. His income chaos wasn't about technical capability—his expertise was solid. What was missing was any visible pattern in how he delivered it. Each engagement felt invented from scratch.

"I stopped assuming every client needed a completely different approach," he reflected. "The recognition was uncomfortable—but also a relief."

What the Chaos Hides

Even with the identity shift from Part One, certain patterns keep the real issues invisible.

Communication inconsistency makes it impossible to see what you're actually doing. When you respond immediately sometimes and take days other times, you can't distinguish between what works and what doesn't. The chaos obscures what's actually happening.

Avoiding looking at what actually generates results keeps everything theoretical. When you don't track which activities produce revenue, improvement has nowhere to start. The absence of information masquerades as the absence of anything to see.

Treating each project as isolated prevents you from seeing natural progressions. When every engagement ends completely, you can't recognize where relationships might continue.

Keeping everything in your head prevents you from seeing what you're actually doing.

When nothing gets documented, you can't tell what's repeating versus what's truly necessary.

The fifth client engagement wasn't easier because I had more experience. It was easier because I knew exactly what I was walking into, what I would need, and what the end looked like.

That single page of documentation didn't constrain the work. It freed me to do it.

That is the shift this chapter is pointing toward: not better effort, but work that no longer has to be reinvented every time.

Reliability isn't a personality trait. It's a system.

Chapter 8: No Longer Invented From Scratch

Chaos doesn't come from effort. It comes from work that never becomes repeatable.

The fifth client was David. He had been a renovation contractor in Durham for nineteen years, and his coordination problem wasn't complicated: The cabinetry supplier, the electrician, and the countertop installer never talked to each other. Every question came through David personally.

I had solved this exact problem four times. I had different notes for each one—a different approach, a different sequence, a different format for the handoff. I had been treating my expertise like a custom art project. Each time, from scratch. The problem wasn't new. The clients changed. The building specifications changed. The core problem didn't.

Sitting in David's truck outside the site, working through my disorganized file, I finally let myself see it fully. I had been an engineer for more than twenty years. I didn't approach structural problems by inventing a new method each time. I applied tested approaches, documented what worked, and built on what had been learned.

But in my own consulting work, I was still starting from zero every time.

The Page That Changed the Work

The deeper version of this recognition came earlier, during a construction coordination project in Singapore.

I was younger in my international career then, still operating under the assumption that being indispensable required being present. Design revisions moved quickly on that project. Contractors needed answers. Project managers expected immediate clarification. If I was unavailable for even an afternoon, decisions stalled.

So I stayed available. Every question came through me. Every clarification required a conversation. The work moved—but only as fast as I could respond.

Then something changed.

After one particularly chaotic week, I began leaving written markup packages with each revision—clear notes, sketches, step-by-step annotations explaining exactly what had changed and why. Nothing sophisticated. Just clearer documentation.

The effect was immediate. Fewer interruptions. Fewer repeated questions. Contractors began coordinating among themselves before coming back to me.

What I had assumed required constant presence turned out to require something else.

Clarity.

That was the first time I understood the shift. My value wasn't in being available. It was in making the expertise visible and usable without me.

What the Notes Revealed

Back in Durham, sitting in David's truck, I recognized the same gap. I had been applying construction coordination expertise to local contractors. What I hadn't yet done was treat the work the way an engineer treats a method: Test it, document it, refine it, apply it consistently.

The resistance I felt toward structure wasn't professional rigor. It was something quieter. I think I had been afraid that if I wrote down the process too clearly, I would discover it was simpler than I had been making it—that the years of pattern recognition I was selling had a reproducible form, and that reproducibility might somehow reduce its value.

The opposite happened. The clarity forced me to articulate what I actually did, which improved the outcomes. The first page of documentation I handed David before signing—a single sheet describing the three phases, what I would need from him, and what the final handoff would look like—produced something I hadn't expected. He signed the scope the same day. Previous clients had taken two or three weeks. They had been making decisions in the dark. The clarity wasn't mine alone.

The transition is not always smooth. Treating your own expertise as something systematic rather than intuitive requires confronting the possibility that intuition has been doing more work than you realized—and that the work it was doing can be made visible and transferable. That is a useful confrontation to have. It doesn't happen all at once. It begins with one page.

Every Case Is Different

What I learned through David's project, and through Singapore before it, is that earning changes shape before it stabilizes.

The first shift is from irregular to reliable—from income that appears unpredictably to income that arrives because you have built a method that produces it. The second shift, smaller and easier to miss, is from reliable to repeatable—from work that runs because you're present to work that runs because you have made the method clear enough to function without your constant reinvention of it.

That second shift is where earning stops feeling like a chase.

When you find yourself saying "every case is different," pause. Sometimes that sentence describes reality. Often it protects you from seeing a pattern that is already repeatable—and from the small discomfort of writing it down.

After Earning Stabilizes

There is a third problem, one that reliable income doesn't solve and repeatable delivery doesn't address. It's the problem of what happens to money once it arrives.

Most people assume that once they're earning consistently, the anxiety will ease. It rarely does on its own. The Smart Struggle Loop doesn't disappear when the income stabilizes. It relocates. The same analytical mind that once spent four days comparing savings account interest rates begins instead to monitor balances obsessively, track every outflow, and watch something that is, in fact, already working.

The watching becomes the problem.

Reactive Money vs Flowing Money

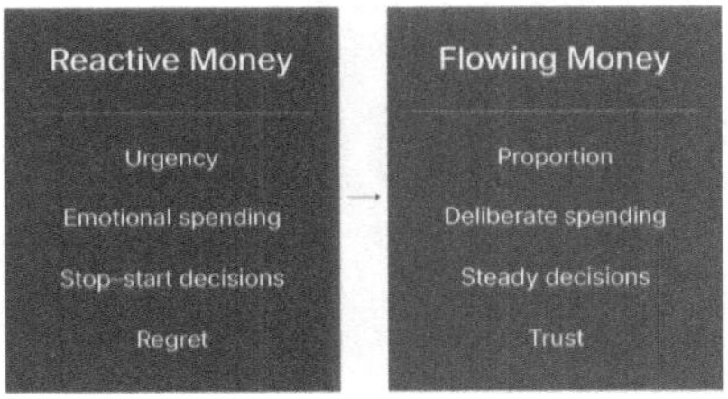

What changes when money stops being reactive.

Interlude: Migration

The problem changes shape before it goes away.

For a while, it looks like progress. Income stabilizes. The pressure eases.

Then attention shifts.

Not to earning more—to making sure nothing slips. Watching balances. Tracking movement. Checking what was already decided.

The Loop doesn't disappear. It reorganizes.

Watch what happens when management becomes monitoring.

PART THREE: MANAGING

Reliable income does not end the Loop. It changes where the Loop appears.

Chapter 9: When Stability Still Feels Unsafe

Income is not the same problem as money.

Most people discover this around the time the income problem stabilizes and the anxiety doesn't. Same amount arriving. Same tightening at 2 a.m. Different source.

Once income becomes reliable, the anxiety often changes form. It moves from earning the money to watching the money.

It shows up quietly at first. You open your banking app once in the morning, just to check. Nothing urgent. By lunch, you check again. By evening, you've opened it four times—not because anything changed, but because something in you is looking for confirmation that everything is still okay.

Jessica woke up at 2 a.m. in a panic. Had she transferred money for tomorrow's mortgage? Was her business account high enough for payroll?

The mental load was exhausting. Income existed. Systems worked. But every dollar still needed her attention.

If you've built earning systems but still spend hours managing where money goes, this is the next problem to address.

Six months later, Jessica's money moves automatically. Bills pay themselves. Savings accumulate. Taxes are set aside. She has stopped carrying money management in her head.

Even if "money automation" sounds complicated or risky, you're not building complex systems from scratch. You're using simple tools that most banks offer for free to eliminate the constant mental burden of manual money management. The complexity is in the strategy, not the technology.

Control Through Design

You've built earning systems that generate money more reliably. The next challenge is making that money work without constant attention. This chapter begins that shift from income to infrastructure.

The resistance to automation sounds responsible: I need to watch my money closely to stay in control. But the reality is the reverse. Manual management traps your attention in constant supervision. Automation creates control through design.

The Cost of Manual Control

Manual money management creates four predictable problems even when income is reliable:

Mental burden means constant tracking of balances, bills, and deadlines consumes attention that could focus on earning or living. The cognitive load drains energy without creating value.

Financial stress narrows attention. Research on cognitive scarcity shows that when money demands constant monitoring, it consumes mental bandwidth that would otherwise go to work, planning, and ordinary life.[1]

Timing errors happen when you forget deadlines, miss transfers, or accidentally overdraw accounts because you're tracking too many moving parts manually. These mistakes cost money through late fees and create unnecessary stress.

Reactive allocation means money sits in checking accounts waiting for your attention instead of moving automatically to where it serves you best. You know you should be saving and investing, but "I'll do it this weekend" becomes "I'll do it next month" becomes "I haven't saved anything this year."

How Automated Money Systems Work

Money automation transforms manual management into lower-stress systems through four components that work together.

One Balance, Five Questions

The first component is account architecture—designing an account structure that separates operational money, protective reserves, and wealth-building funds.

Financial stress research demonstrates that cognitive resources automatically captured by money anxiety reduce mental capacity available for productive work and decision-making.

1. Sendhil Mullainathan and Eldar Shafir, Scarcity: Why Having Too Little Means So Much (New York: Times Books, 2013).

Most people use one or two accounts for everything, which makes systematic management impossible. Clear separation enables automation.

Jessica had been using one checking account and one savings account because it felt simpler, but the simplicity was deceptive. One balance was being asked to answer every money question at once: what could be spent, what had to be held for bills, what belonged to taxes, what protected her from disruption, and what could be moved toward long-term growth. The account structure didn't add complexity. It made the existing complexity visible enough to manage.

Each category of money had one job. Operating money handled income and immediate expenses, with a small buffer for ordinary weekly life. Bill money stayed separate so recurring obligations didn't compete with daily spending. Tax reserves prevented self-employed income from feeling larger than it really was. Emergency money protected the system from disruption. Wealth-building money moved the future out of intention and into structure.

Once each account had a job, Jessica no longer had to interpret the same balance every day. Income arrived, transfers moved automatically, and the system replaced constant manual judgment with visible flow. The point wasn't to create more accounts for the sake of organization. The point was to stop asking a single account balance to answer five different questions at once.

Start with your current accounts and list every monetary account you currently have. Identify what each one does versus what you intended it to do.

Define clear purposes by writing a specific purpose for each account. If you can't articulate clear purpose, you probably don't need that account.

Eliminate redundancy by closing accounts that serve no distinct purpose. Having eight accounts with vague intentions creates complexity without benefit.

Most people need four to six accounts maximum. One for income/operations, one for bills, one for tax reserves if self-employed, one for emergency fund, one for wealth building, possibly one for business.

Common mistakes: creating too many accounts with overlapping purposes. Using one account for everything, making automation impossible.

I resisted this structure for a year. Five accounts felt like overkill. Manual tracking failed repeatedly. I overspent from my Operating account because discretionary funds weren't separated.

What finally convinced me wasn't theory. It was repetition.

The same mistake kept returning in different forms—bills paid late not from crisis, but from attention drift; money held in the wrong place because I wanted everything visible at once; the false feeling of control that came from watching rather than designing.

The structure didn't create complexity. It exposed the complexity I was already carrying manually.

When the System Meets Real Life

The system was tested within the first three months. Not by a crisis, but by something more ordinary and therefore more revealing: the friction any new structure encounters when it meets the irregularity of actual life.

In the second month of the automation, a scheduled transfer from my Operating account to my Tax Reserve account didn't go through. I didn't notice immediately. The bank had flagged the account for a routine verification after a recent address update and had placed a hold on automated transfers while the verification was processed. No notification reached me. The transfer simply didn't happen.

I discovered it six days later during my weekly check. By then, a client payment had arrived and been partially reallocated by the subsequent automated transfers, but because the tax reserve transfer hadn't run, the percentages were off. The Operating account held more than it should have. The Tax Reserve account held less.

My first response was the old one: The system failed; this is why you should watch it more closely; this is why daily checking feels safer.

My second response arrived more slowly and was different in kind. The system had surfaced the error within a week. The error was correctable. Nothing catastrophic had happened.

I called the bank, resolved the verification hold, manually transferred the correct amount to the Tax Reserve account, and documented what had happened so I would recognize it if it recurred. The whole thing took about forty minutes.

What mattered about those forty minutes wasn't the task itself, but the order in which things happened. In the past, discovering an error like that would have triggered shame before solution: You should have caught this; you're not paying close enough attention; this is what happens when you trust systems. I would have spent energy managing the self-accusation before I addressed the actual problem.

This time, the problem and the solution arrived in the same frame. The system hadn't collapsed. It had encountered an external obstacle, made the discrepancy visible within a reasonable interval, and left me with something specific and correctable. That wasn't failure. That was a functioning structure meeting real-world friction.

Auditing, Not Watching

A different lesson took longer to learn. In the early weeks of automation, there is a discomfort that doesn't get described very clearly: the discomfort of trusting a system that is working. When the transfers ran correctly, when the bills were paid on time, when the tax reserve filled up, when the emergency fund grew, there was nothing to do. No error to correct. No problem to solve. And that absence of problem felt wrong. My nervous system had been trained by years of manual management to interpret constant attention as care. Not paying attention felt, at first, like neglect.

The weekly check mattered because it gave the attention a boundary. I wasn't ignoring my finances. I was attending to them deliberately, on a schedule, rather than compulsively and without pattern. The distinction seemed small at first. Over time, it became essential.

The engineer in me eventually found a frame for it that helped. I was no longer monitoring the system. I was auditing it. Monitoring is continuous surveillance, appropriate for systems that require constant human intervention. Auditing is periodic verification, appropriate for systems designed to run autonomously. My money system had become something closer to the second category. Treating it as though it still required constant supervision was not diligence. It was a failure to trust the design.

When the Reserve Does Its Job

About ten months into the system, my car required roughly two thousand dollars in repairs. Unexpected, yes, but not catastrophic. In earlier years, that expense would have gone onto a credit card and then remained there for several months while I worked to pay it down.

This time, the expense came out of the emergency fund. I transferred the amount, had the car repaired, and set up an automatic replenishment schedule to rebuild the reserve over the following three months.

The important change wasn't the transaction itself. It was how the event was experienced. I had expected the repair to feel like a setback. Instead, it felt like evidence. The system had been designed to absorb exactly this kind of event, and when the event arrived, it did. That wasn't luck. It was the structure functioning as intended.

A few days later, I was sitting at the kitchen table with coffee and had a thought that wouldn't have been available to me in earlier years: The car needed work, we handled it, we are rebuilding the reserve, and nothing has been derailed.

That sentence mattered because in the past there had been no clean way to absorb an interruption. Every unexpected expense had felt like a system failure because there had been no real system. There had only been ongoing improvisation.

The reserve changed the category of the problem. It moved an emergency into the space of a manageable inconvenience. That shift wasn't only about the money. It was about the design.

Money That Moves Without You

The second component is automatic money flow—setting up systematic transfers that move money to correct accounts without manual intervention.

Once account architecture exists, automation ensures money flows correctly whether you're paying attention or not.

Jessica's percentages were not universal targets. They reflected her income pattern, tax obligations, expenses, and business structure.

Jessica's transfers moved money on income arrival: 30% to Tax Reserve, 15% to Emergency Fund, 10% to Discretionary, and the remainder stayed in Operating before being distributed to the Bills account and business expenses.

From Operating to the Bills account, she transferred a fixed monthly amount covering all recurring bills plus 15% buffer for variable expenses.

This systematic flow meant money moved correctly whether Jessica was paying attention or not. Income arrived and automatically split to serve different purposes. She never had to think about "move money to savings this week" because it happened automatically.

To find your own percentages, review three to six months of actual income and expenses, then choose allocations that fit your obligations, volatility, and current capacity. Identify realistic allocation percentages based on your situation, not theoretical ideals.

Starting conservative works well. If you're not sure what percentages work, starting lower and increasing gradually is more sustainable than planning aggressive transfers you'll have to reverse constantly.

Most banks allow scheduled or triggered transfers. Set up automatic transfers from Operating to other accounts using percentage-based rules if your income varies, or fixed amounts if income is consistent.

Building in flexibility helps. Life happens. Set up transfers you can pause if needed, while making pausing require conscious decision rather than defaulting to manual control.

Irregular income adjustment: If income varies significantly month-to-month, percentage-based transfers triggered by deposits work better than fixed amounts on fixed dates. When $2,000 arrive, percentages move automatically. When $5,000 arrive, percentages adjust automatically to the larger amount.

If automation feels risky, start with one transfer—even $25 weekly to savings proves the system works. You can increase amounts after you trust the process.

The Belief Beneath Manual Control

That resistance to automation is the Smart Struggle Loop in its management form. The Loop is no longer asking for more research; it is asking for more manual control. The belief underneath it is simple: "If I keep touching the money, I stay safe." But touching is not the same as directing. The more you manage every movement by hand, the more your sense of safety depends on staying involved. Automation interrupts that pattern by moving the decision out of the anxious moment and into a system you designed when you were clear.

The resistance had one sentence: "What if I need that money after it's moved?" It kept me managing manually for years.

Bills Without Background Noise

The third component is bill payment automation—eliminating deadline tracking by automating recurring obligations.

Every bill you pay manually consumes mental energy and creates risk of missed payments. Automation eliminates both problems.

Jessica automated all recurring bills:

Fixed bills, same amount monthly: rent, insurance premiums, subscription services, loan payments. Set to autopay from Bills account.

Variable bills, amount changes monthly: utilities, phone, internet. Set to autopay from Bills account. Jessica checked statements quarterly but didn't track monthly.

Irregular bills, annual or quarterly: car registration, professional licenses, software renewals. Added to Bills account monthly allocation, divided by 12.

Before you automate anything, list every recurring obligation—monthly, quarterly, annual. Include the subscriptions you have vague awareness of but haven't looked at directly in months. This step almost always reveals something you forgot you were paying for. That is useful information before the automation runs, not after.

The mechanics are straightforward: most vendors offer autopay, and most banks allow scheduled transfers that you set once and don't touch again. The structural choice that matters is timing. If your income arrives on the first and fifteenth, bills scheduled shortly after those dates will draw from accounts that are actually funded. Bills scheduled mid-cycle, when the account may be lower, will occasionally fail. This failure isn't a system problem. It's a timing problem, and it's entirely avoidable.

One precaution earns its weight: Keep a 10–15% buffer in your Bills account beyond the expected monthly total. Utility bills spike. Insurance premiums recalculate. A buffer absorbs the irregular without triggering anything you have to manage manually.

The mistake I made in the first months of automation was treating "set it" as the same thing as "forget it." I checked my banking app constantly. Engineers are trained to monitor systems, not trust them. Every transfer felt like something I should verify.

Over time, I learned that a quarterly review—ten minutes, not a deep audit—was enough. It confirmed that the autopay list still reflected what I actually used, that no billing error had been quietly compounding, and that rates on recurring services hadn't drifted past the point of being worth revisiting. The automation runs without you. The review is how you stay the one in charge of it.

Nothing failed. Bills paid on schedule. Transfers happened exactly when they were supposed to.

The surprising change wasn't financial—it was psychological. The mental space that had been spent tracking balances and deadlines simply disappeared.

Instead of reviewing accounts at night, I was spending that time with my family or focusing on client work. That was enough.

The Sunday evenings I had spent reconciling accounts, I gave back to my family. Not dramatically. We didn't do anything special with them. We just had them—unscheduled, unmonitored, without the background calculation that had been running through every unstructured hour for years.

That was the measurement I hadn't known to track.

The Buffer Between Surprise and Crisis

The fourth component is emergency reserves—building protective cash reserves automatically so unexpected expenses don't derail progress.

Emergency reserves create resilience. They're the buffer between "unexpected expense" and "financial crisis." Without reserves, every surprise becomes an emergency requiring debt or derailing your wealth building.

Jessica built her emergency fund systematically:

Target: three months of essential expenses initially, expanding to six months as income stabilized. She calculated actual essential expenses, not ideal budget: housing, utilities, food, insurance, minimum loan payments. Her three-month target was $9,000. Her six-month target was $18,000.

Contribution schedule: $500 monthly automatic transfer from Operating to Emergency Fund. In high-income months, she transferred operating surplus as well.

Timeline: Reached three-month reserve in eighteen months. Reached six-month reserve fourteen months after that.

Use policy: Emergency Fund was for genuine emergencies only—job loss, major unexpected expenses, significant income disruption. Not for "I want this" purchases or "this would be convenient" spending.

This reserve transformed Jessica's financial psychology from constant anxiety to calm confidence.

Calculate your target by listing true essential monthly expenses. Multiply by 3 for initial target, 6 for full reserve.

Essential expenses include housing: rent, mortgage, property tax, insurance; utilities; food; transportation; insurance premiums; and minimum debt payments.

Essential expenses don't include dining out, entertainment, subscriptions, shopping, hobbies, upgrades, or convenience expenses.

Most people overestimate essential expenses by including lifestyle preferences as necessities. Your emergency reserve is for survival, not maintaining your current lifestyle perfectly.

Set a realistic contribution based on your automatic money flow. Determine what you can contribute monthly, starting with an amount you can sustain indefinitely rather than an aggressive amount you'll abandon after three months.

Build gradually: If you can only contribute $100 monthly, that's $1,200 annually. In three years, you'll have $3,600—which covers many emergencies and is infinitely better than zero. Perfect shouldn't prevent good enough.

Separate the account: Keep emergency reserves in a separate account you don't access casually. High-yield savings accounts are good options—easy to access in genuine emergency, not connected to your daily spending accounts.

Building an emergency fund felt slow. Saving $200 monthly took years to reach three months of expenses. When unexpected $2,400 car repairs hit, I charged it and paid interest for months. Even $3,000 in reserves would have saved that cost and stress.

Trusting the Design

My turning point wasn't when I earned more—it was when I designed a system that removed my attention from day-to-day operations. Once money began moving automatically, the stress eased faster than my income changed.

The breakthrough came when I finally implemented account architecture and automation. I set up separate accounts for operations, bills, taxes, emergency fund, and wealth building. I automated transfers so money moved systematically whether I was paying attention or not. I automated bill payments so deadlines disappeared from my mental tracking.

The result wasn't just better financial outcomes—though I did save more and eliminate late fees. The result was mental freedom. I stopped thinking about money constantly because the systems handled operations automatically. I could focus on earning and living rather than tracking and managing.

The shift reminded me of engineering principles: Good systems require thoughtful design but minimal ongoing management. Poor systems demand constant attention and still produce inferior results. Money operations follow identical principles.

The hardest part wasn't setting up the automation—banks make that relatively simple. At first I still checked the accounts frequently out of habit. The systems worked exactly as designed. My attention had been the problem, not the solution.

When you find yourself checking balances obsessively, ask: Am I managing money or preventing myself from trusting my systems? The attention feels like diligence but blocks the automation's purpose.

If automating your money feels like losing control or seems risky, that's normal. Most people resist money automation because it feels like money is moving without their permission. But automation gives you more control by ensuring money moves according to your priorities rather than your impulses or forgetfulness.

Where the Setup Breaks Down

Automating without buffers sets up automatic transfers and payments without maintaining buffer balances in relevant accounts, leading to overdrafts when timing misaligns. The fix: Keep one month's bills as buffer in your Bills account. Maintain one to two weeks' operating expenses in your Operating account.

Over-automating initially sets up complex multi-account systems with aggressive transfers before testing at smaller scale, creating failure when reality doesn't match plans. The fix: Start with basic structure and conservative transfers. Add complexity and increase amounts gradually after proving the system works.

Not reviewing periodically means setting automation and never checking again, missing billing errors, rate increases, or changing circumstances that require adjustment. The fix: Review all automated operations quarterly. Adjust as needed based on actual results.

Keeping all money accessible means having emergency reserves in checking accounts or easily accessible locations, making them psychologically available for non-emergency uses. The fix: Put emergency reserves in a separate account at a different institution if necessary to create friction preventing casual access.

Automating bills without tracking the Bills account means setting bills on autopay without ensuring the account stays funded through automatic transfers, leading to overdrafts. The fix: Automate both sides—automatic transfers funding the Bills account plus automatic payments from it. Check the balance quarterly.

These mistakes cost real money. Aggressive savings automation without buffer meant reversing transfers and paying fees. Bill automation without balance verification triggered expensive overdrafts.

Automation isn't about technology.

It's about trust in your design, not your discipline.

Money automation transforms manual management into lower-stress operations through four integrated components.

Jessica went from constant money stress and manual tracking to automated calm. The setup took ninety days, then the system continued running over the months that followed.

You're becoming someone who manages money through systematic automation rather than constant manual intervention.

The resistance you feel to automation—"I need to watch my money closely to stay in control"—inverts reality. Real control comes from building systems that keep working when your attention is elsewhere, not from vigilance that exhausts you.

The money did not become safer. The relationship became honest. Those aren't the same thing. Only one of them is within your control.

Chapter 10: The Delay That Looks Like Research

The Decision He Kept Deferring

Complexity feels responsible right up to the point where it becomes a hiding place.

In investing, delay rarely looks like avoidance. It looks like intelligence working at full capacity.

You compare platforms. You read fund descriptions. You watch three different explanations of the same concept, just to be sure you're not missing something. Each step feels responsible. Each step feels like progress.

But the decision itself never arrives.

Investment paralysis usually isn't a knowledge problem. It is what happens when complexity gives delay a respectable disguise.

George had $8,000 in savings. For six months, he had been telling himself, "I need to start investing," while doing nothing. Every time he researched, the options multiplied—target-date funds, index funds, individual stocks, bonds, robo-advisors. Each option seemed to require a different set of concepts. The research felt productive, but it kept action at a distance.

That was the trap. The more seriously he treated the decision, the easier it became to postpone it.

If you recognize that trap, you should. Where I once spent days comparing savings accounts that differed by a fraction of a percent, George spent months comparing investment options that all, in the end, required the same first step: Open the account. The story his mind was running—"I need to understand everything before I can act safely"—wasn't preparation. It was complexity protecting hesitation.

The cost of that postponement is easy to miss because nothing dramatic happens at first. The money stays visible. The account feels safe. The loss is quiet.

Money sitting in savings earns very little. Inflation quietly erodes its value over time. If inflation runs at 3% and your savings earn 0.5%, you lose 2.5% of real value each year without noticing. At 0.5%, $10,000 becomes about $11,600 in thirty years. At 10%, the same $10,000 becomes about $174,000. The gap isn't subtle. It's the difference between preservation and growth.

George understood this in theory. That understanding wasn't enough to produce action.

For months, he researched investment accounts without opening one. The more he learned, the more complicated the decision seemed. Each new concept created another reason to wait. He built comparison spreadsheets he never used. He bookmarked articles he read twice and then forgot. He told himself he was getting closer to ready when he was actually getting further from starting. The barrier wasn't complexity. It was knowing enough to hesitate—and not enough to act.

The shift began when he stopped trying to understand everything at once and focused on making one decision he could actually execute.

He opened the account.

George simplified the decision by looking at three broad account categories. His starting question wasn't which fund to buy. It was which type of account he needed to understand first.

Retirement accounts provide tax advantages for long-term savings. Specific names vary by country, but the core structures remain consistent. There are two main types, and the difference matters.

Some accounts reduce your taxable income today. You contribute before tax, the money grows, and you pay tax when you withdraw it later. This works well if you expect to be in a lower tax bracket in retirement.

Others work the opposite way. You contribute after-tax money, it grows tax-free, and qualified withdrawals later are also tax-free. This structure offers greater flexibility and works well if your tax rate is likely to stay the same or rise.

For most people starting out, the uncertainty of future tax rates makes flexibility valuable. George chose the tax-free structure as his primary account.

He also contributed to his employer-sponsored retirement plan up to the company match. Employer matching is an immediate, guaranteed return before any market performance.

He used accounts without tax advantages—which have fewer restrictions but no tax benefits—only after the tax-advantaged options were maximized.

Three accounts. Clear purposes. Nothing more.

He opened the account through a low-cost provider. The decision he had spent months overthinking took minutes to execute.

A Structure He Could Follow

The next problem appeared immediately.

Once the account existed, he had to decide what to invest in. Asset allocation determines outcomes more than individual investment selection. The decision isn't which specific stock to choose. It is how to distribute money across asset types—stocks, bonds, and other instruments—with different levels of growth and volatility.

Stocks represent ownership in companies. Over long periods they have produced higher returns, but with significant short-term fluctuations—gains or losses of 20 to 30 percent in a single year aren't unusual. Bonds represent loans to governments or corporations, offering lower returns with more stability. The balance between them determines how much your portfolio grows during strong periods and how much it falls during weak ones.

George initially tried to understand every allocation strategy before choosing one. He read about age-based rules, three-fund portfolios, factor investing, international diversification ratios. Every strategy had advocates. Every strategy had critics. That approach produced the same result as before: delay.

The turning point came when he realized he didn't need the optimal allocation. He needed a structure he would actually follow.

He chose a target-date fund aligned with his expected retirement year.

A target-date fund is a single fund that holds a broad mix of investments and adjusts its allocation automatically over time. When the target year is far away, it usually holds more growth-oriented assets. As the target year approaches, it gradually shifts toward a more conservative allocation. The fund handles rebalancing according to its design. For George, the value was not that he could ignore what he owned. The value was that the structure reduced the number of decisions he had to remake every month. He still needed to understand the basic risks, costs, and assumptions behind the fund, but he no longer needed to turn every market movement into a new decision.

One fund. Broad diversification. Automatic rebalancing over time. No ongoing decisions required.

The complexity didn't disappear. It was handled by the structure.

Once the allocation decision was made, the remaining step was consistency.

Manual investing fails in predictable ways. Contributions are skipped during busy months. Timing decisions interfere—waiting for the market to drop before buying, or for more certainty before committing. Emotions drive irregular behavior—investing heavily during confidence and stopping during uncertainty. Every one of these behaviors reduces long-term returns. Not occasionally. Reliably.

George removed those decisions.

He set up an automatic transfer of $500 per month from his wealth-building account into his long-term investment account on the fifth of each month, two days after his income arrived. The funds were automatically invested into a single, diversified fund. The system ran without requiring attention.

He didn't need to decide when to invest. He didn't need to interpret market conditions. He only needed to let the system continue.

The amount mattered less than the start. Even a small, consistent contribution was enough to establish the system. Automation made the decision once and removed the need to make it again.

The Test Was Staying

Several months into this process, the test arrived.

The market dropped.

His portfolio declined by 15 percent in a matter of weeks. The number on the screen moved downward quickly enough to trigger a familiar response.

Stop. Protect what remains. Avoid further loss.

The instinct felt rational. It wasn't.

He paused. The story was immediate: I'm losing money. The fact was different: Markets fluctuate. Declines are part of long-term growth. His strategy hadn't changed. A 15 percent decline was uncomfortable, but it was not unusual. Long-term investors eventually experience periods when account values fall sharply enough to make staying invested feel irrational. These aren't failures of the system. They are the system operating normally.

The automated contributions continued. Each monthly investment purchased shares at lower prices during the decline. He was buying more of the same fund for the same $500—more units, lower cost, same destination.

In George's example, the market recovered within a few months, and the shares purchased during the decline later increased in value. In other periods, recovery can take much longer. The point is not that every decline resolves quickly, or that volatility feels like an opportunity while it is happening. The point is that a working system can keep fear from remaking the decision in the middle of a downturn. George had done neither of the things his anxiety wanted him to do: he had not stopped the system, and he had not sold in panic. The system had not failed. It had done what it was designed to do.

The hardest part of long-term investing isn't the setup. It's the staying. The system made staying the default, and departing from it a deliberate choice that required effort. That friction wasn't incidental. It was the point.

The Difference Was Continuity

By the end of the first year, nothing about George's investment approach had become more complex. He hadn't learned advanced financial theory. He hadn't begun analyzing markets or adjusting his strategy based on news. He had implemented a structure and allowed it to operate. The difference wasn't knowledge. It was continuity.

When I first started accumulating savings from consulting work, I kept everything in high-yield savings accounts. I knew I should be investing but delayed the decision, convinced I needed to understand more before acting.

Part of that delay was the Loop—the same research-as-avoidance pattern I had been running for years. But part of it was older. I had grown up in a world where money held in savings was money you could see, and money invested was money you had trusted to forces you couldn't control. The instinct toward protection had made sense when circumstances were genuinely uncertain. It had simply never updated when the circumstances changed.

The barrier wasn't complexity. It was hesitation reinforced by the appearance of prudence. Avoiding investment risk felt responsible. In reality, it guaranteed loss through inflation. My caution wasn't conservative. It was costly.

The shift came when I stopped treating investing as a skill that required expertise and recognized it as a system that required consistency. In engineering, we use proven methods and established standards rather than inventing custom solutions for routine problems. Investing works the same way. Proven structures already exist. They don't require constant adjustment. They require implementation.

When research becomes a substitute for action, complexity becomes expensive.

These patterns repeat across most failed attempts at investing. Research replaces execution. Complexity delays commitment. Timing replaces consistency. The investors who build wealth aren't those who answered every question correctly. They are the ones who stopped letting the questions delay the first step.

How Money Gets Stuck

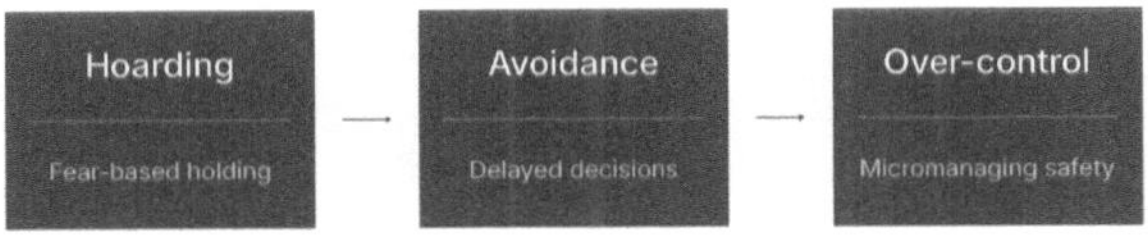

Common ways we unintentionally block money flow.

Complexity isn't the enemy of wealth. It becomes dangerous when it gives the Smart Struggle Loop a respectable place to hide. As long as George was comparing platforms, reading fund descriptions, and waiting to understand one more detail, he could feel responsible while the account stayed empty.

The solution wasn't to become careless. It was to choose a structure simple enough to begin and steady enough to continue. A broad fund, an automatic transfer, and a decision made before the next wave of research could reopen the Loop gave him something complexity had never given him: continuity.

That is what a working investment system does for an analytical mind. It removes the need to keep proving readiness. Once the decision is designed, repeated action no longer depends on repeated courage, and doing nothing begins to mean something different. It no longer means avoidance. It means the system is finally working.

Chapter 11: The Structure of Debt

The Spreadsheet She Avoided

Three years ago, Elena stared at her debt spreadsheet: $23,784 in credit cards, $15,000 in a personal loan, $8,000 remaining on a car loan.

Total: $46,784.

The minimum payments consumed $985 each month—money that could have been building wealth was instead tied up in debt repayment.

She had tried to eliminate debt before. For a few months, she would make aggressive payments, pushing balances down with intensity. Then something small—a car repair, a medical bill, a shift in income—would interrupt the effort. The extra payments stopped. The balances stabilized. Progress reversed.

Over time, the debt stopped feeling like a problem.

It felt like a fact. Something that existed in the background, quietly shaping every financial decision she made.

This was also the same Elena who had been learning to open her banking app with shaking hands instead of waiting for the fear to pass. The $847.22 she had finally forced herself to look at months earlier was only her checking account balance, not the full debt picture. This spreadsheet was the rest of the picture—the debt structure she hadn't yet turned toward. She had practiced catching her body's signal—the chest tightening, the breath going shallow—before it became full shutdown. She had recognized how quickly her mind filled with reasons to postpone any financial action that might show her something she didn't want to see.

She had done all of that work. And she was still carrying $46,784 in debt.

This is the part recognition doesn't resolve. Naming the Loop interrupts it, but it doesn't clear what the Loop has already built. The debt was structural. What changed was how she could approach it—without the long avoidance that used to come first, and with the ability to stay in the room once the numbers were visible. The work ahead was no longer about insight. It was about reduction.

What the Debt Was Doing

The numbers told a different story than the one she had been living with.

Her credit cards alone were costing her about $450 per month in interest—more than $5,400 per year transferred out of her finances without reducing the balances in any meaningful way. A $10,000 balance at 22% interest, making only minimum payments, can stretch into decades of repayment. The total cost can more than double. Time becomes the multiplier.

At the same time, every dollar sent to interest is a dollar that can't be invested. Three hundred dollars per month redirected into investments earning 8% could grow to more than $400,000 over thirty years. The cost of debt isn't only what you pay. It is what you never get the chance to build.

Debt occupies cognitive bandwidth in the background, narrowing the mental space available for long-term planning and decision-making.[1]

When the voice says "I'll never get out of debt" or "I should have been smarter about borrowing," that is a trigger. The story is "debt means I'm financially irresponsible." The fact is different: debt is a system running in the wrong direction. Not a character flaw. A structural problem.

The List She Finally Made

For two years, Elena avoided writing down all of her debts in one place.

She knew the numbers individually. She didn't want to see them collectively.

When she finally listed everything—every balance, every interest rate, every minimum payment—the total was higher than she expected. The reaction was familiar. Shame. Not because the numbers had changed, but because they were now visible.

But the numbers weren't judgment. They were structure.

Her inventory looked like this: Credit Card 1: $9,184 at 24.99%, $173 minimum; Credit Card 2: $6,200 at 21.49%, $124 minimum; Credit Card 3: $4,800 at 19.99%, $96 minimum; Credit Card 4:

1. Mullainathan and Shafir, Scarcity.

$3,600 at 22.99%, $72 minimum; Personal Loan: $15,000 at 11.5%, $320 minimum; Car Loan: $8,000 at 6.5%, $200 minimum.

Total: $46,784. Minimum payments: $985 per month.

For the first time, the problem was no longer abstract. It was defined.

I had avoided the same step. For months I told myself I "basically knew" what I owed. When I finally listed everything precisely, the total was $8,000 higher than I had been carrying in my head. That gap—between what was real and what I allowed myself to acknowledge—was where inaction lived. Vague awareness keeps debt in place. Precise clarity makes it actionable.

Most people don't avoid their debt because they don't care. They avoid it because they already know enough to feel overwhelmed.

You have a rough number in your head. You know which balances are the worst. You've seen enough statements to understand the direction. But you don't sit down and look at it all at once.

That's the Loop again. Not ignorance—partial knowledge feeding avoidance. The mind circles the edges of the problem because seeing the full shape would require a decision.

So the system never gets built, not because you don't know how—but because the Loop never lets the problem become fully visible long enough to act on it.

The Money Had a Direction

Once the full picture was visible, the next decision wasn't how to eliminate everything at once. It was where to begin.

Not all debt behaves the same way. Interest rates vary. Some balances grow faster than others. Left unstructured, payments spread thinly across multiple accounts, reducing nothing meaningfully.

Two proven sequencing strategies exist, each with different strengths.

The avalanche method targets the highest interest rate first—mathematically optimal, saving the most money in interest over time. Elena's sequence would run: Credit Card 1 at 24.99%, Credit Card 4 at 22.99%, Credit Card 2 at 21.49%, Credit Card 3 at 19.99%, then the personal loan, then the car loan.

The snowball method targets the smallest balance first—psychologically motivating, creating early wins that build momentum. Elena's sequence would run differently: Credit Card 4 at $3,600, Credit Card 3 at $4,800, Credit Card 2 at $6,200, then the car loan, then Credit Card 1 at $9,184, then the personal loan.

Both methods work. The question is which one you will actually follow. If your interest rates are similar and you need early wins to stay motivated, snowball. If the rate differences are significant and efficiency matters more than psychology, avalanche.

Elena's highest-rate card cost nearly four times more than her car loan. She chose avalanche. The interest rate difference made the mathematical case too clear to ignore.

She continued making minimum payments on all accounts. Every additional dollar went to Credit Card 1.

Progress at first was slow. Then something shifted.

When the first card was eliminated, its payment didn't disappear. It moved. The $173 minimum, combined with her $800 monthly extra payment, flowed directly into the next balance. The total force attacking that debt increased immediately.

Momentum wasn't created by motivation.

It was created by redirection.

The first balance took eleven months. That was the vulnerable stage, long enough for the old voice to suggest the system wasn't working and that the effort was too slow to matter. Then the first card cleared, and the money that had been trapped in that minimum payment joined the extra payment already aimed at the next balance.

The second debt took four months after that. The third took six. The fourth took five. The remaining debts fell within ten months because the system no longer required Elena to rebuild motivation from zero each time. Each cleared balance increased the force applied to the next one.

The full process took thirty-six months. Making only minimum payments, the same debt would have taken approximately twenty-five years. What compounded was not only the payment force. It was the reversal of the old Loop: avoidance had once made each next step heavier; the system made each next step lighter.

To make this work without relying on willpower month after month, Elena automated the extra payment directly to her highest-priority creditor—set up as a separate transfer beyond the minimum, directed to principal. The decision was made once. The system carried it forward.

She also tracked four numbers on the first of every month: total debt remaining, interest paid that month, number of debts still active, and projected debt-free date. Watching $46,784 become $45,232, then $44,441, then $43,627 created something that willpower alone can't sustain—visible proof that the direction had changed. When the interest paid each month dropped from $657 to $603 to $548, that shrinking number confirmed the system was working even during months when the balance felt stubbornly large. When the count of active debts moved from six to five to four, each reduction felt like a discrete completion—not a step in a process, but a finished thing.

Visibility didn't just track progress. It replaced the need for motivation to do that work.

Relief Without Acceleration

There were points where the system could have collapsed.

Months where the balances didn't move as quickly as expected. Periods where an unexpected expense created pressure to redirect the extra payment toward something else.

And earlier, before she approached it this way, she had tried something different.

She consolidated multiple debts into a single loan with a lower interest rate. The monthly payment dropped. The pressure eased. It felt like progress.

It wasn't.

The lower payment extended the timeline. The total cost increased. Relief without acceleration only stretches the problem over a longer period.

Four patterns derail debt elimination before it gains momentum:

The first is consolidation without acceleration—the one Elena had tried. Lower rate, lower payment, zero urgency to finish.

The second is suspending emergency fund contributions entirely, which works until a car repair or medical bill forces new debt to cover what the emergency fund would have absorbed.

The third is all-or-nothing payment—$800 extra for two months, then a tight month, then stopping and concluding that willpower was the missing ingredient when it was actually a starting amount too aggressive to sustain.

The fourth is eliminating debt while leaving the spending patterns that created it intact. The balance clears. The habits refill it.

I made every one of these mistakes. The most expensive was the consolidation.

I consolidated $18,000 of credit card debt into a personal loan with a lower rate and longer term. The monthly payment dropped from $540 to $380. I felt relief—and then used that breathing room for other spending instead of acceleration. Years passed. The balance remained. The interest rate was lower. The cost was higher. The structure was unchanged, and structure was the only thing that mattered.

What Intensity Couldn't Do

When I finally committed to a system—inventory, avalanche sequence, automated $800 monthly acceleration, monthly tracking—the same income that had produced glacial progress for three years produced $21,000 in eliminated debt within eighteen months.

Not because I earned more. Not because I became more disciplined. Because I stopped treating debt elimination as a willpower challenge and started treating it as a system design problem.

In engineering, inconsistent processes produce inconsistent results regardless of good intentions. Systematic processes produce reliable outcomes because they remove variability. The months I had spent trying to eliminate debt through intention were months where the process was inconsistent and the results confirmed it.

The hardest part wasn't automating the payments. Banks and creditors make that straightforward. The hardest part was facing the complete picture without flinching. The inventory felt like confession. But the debt existed whether I looked at it or not. The inventory simply made it addressable.

Elena's final balance cleared thirty-six months after she created the spreadsheet that once felt too painful to make.

The system had done what intensity alone never could. She didn't eliminate debt by becoming more disciplined. She eliminated it by removing the need for discipline to carry the process.

The constant background tension—calculating, adjusting, worrying—was gone. The absence of that pressure was noticeable only after it disappeared.

A System Moving the Other Way

Debt feels permanent when it is approached without structure. The balances seem too large. The progress seems too slow. The effort feels inconsistent.

What makes it permanent isn't only the amount. It is the absence of a system moving in the opposite direction. Once that system exists, the direction changes. The movement becomes visible. And over time, what once felt fixed begins to change.

Debt isn't a moral failure. It is a system running in the wrong direction. The work is to build one that moves the other way.

Chapter 12: The Risk Left Uncovered

The Policy That Lapsed

Evan spent three years building his financial system.

Income became predictable. Cash flow stabilized. Investments began to grow. Debt was eliminated. The structure worked.

Then his apartment flooded.

Water damage destroyed fifteen thousand dollars' worth of possessions—furniture, electronics, clothing, everything he used daily. He assumed his renter's insurance would cover the loss.

It didn't.

The policy had lapsed six months earlier. He had changed bank accounts during his automation setup and never updated the payment method.

The loss was immediate. Three years of disciplined saving disappeared in a single morning.

The Part He Hadn't Protected

The structure hadn't failed. It had been incomplete.

He had built the part that generates and grows money. He hadn't built the part that protects it.

The gap wasn't visible while everything was working. It became obvious only when something broke.

Unprotected wealth isn't stable. It is exposed.

Asset loss, income disruption, legal liability—these are not rare events. They're normal occurrences that become catastrophic only when no protection exists. A single uninsured event can erase years of progress faster than that progress was built.

Evan had done everything right—except for the part that mattered when something went wrong.

The Four Ways Loss Arrives

Loss comes in four predictable forms:

Physical loss—property destroyed through fire, flood, theft, or accident.

Income loss—work interrupted through illness or injury. Social Security Administration actuarial estimates project that a worker who was insured at age twenty in 2025 has about a 24 percent probability of becoming disabled before normal retirement age. The point is not to predict any one person's future, but to recognize that earning capacity can be interrupted more easily than most people plan for. [1] Many have little or no coverage when it happens.

Liability—being held responsible for damage or harm that leads to financial claims.

And transition failures—errors in how assets transfer or decisions are made during major life events.

These risks are not complex. They are consistent. What varies is whether they are absorbed or amplified.

For years, insurance can feel like an unnecessary expense—money that could be invested instead of paid toward events that may never happen.

Then a situation arises—a misunderstanding, a dispute, a claim that needs to be addressed. Without professional liability coverage, even a minor issue can carry legal costs that far exceed what the premiums would have been.

The events themselves are not exceptional. The absence of structure makes them expensive.

The Coverage That Closed the Gaps

After the loss, Evan rebuilt differently. Not by adding complexity. By closing gaps.

Evan's figures were specific to his situation. They are included as illustration, not as a benchmark. Coverage needs, costs, and legal requirements vary by location, income, assets, family situation, and professional advice.

1. Social Security Administration, Office of the Chief Actuary, Disability and Death Probability Tables for Insured Workers Who Attain Age 20 in 2025, Actuarial Note Number 2025.6, September 2025.

He started with health coverage—ensuring that a medical event wouldn't become a financial crisis. The out-of-pocket maximum mattered more than the premium. His emergency fund from Chapter 9 was sized to cover it.

He extended auto coverage beyond minimum legal requirements. Minimum legal liability limits are typically far below what lawsuits actually cost. Evan chose liability coverage high enough to protect both his current assets and future earnings—about $95 monthly, with collision and uninsured motorist protection added.

Renter's insurance he reinstated immediately. Less than $20 monthly. It would have covered his entire loss. He tied the payment to his primary stable account—not the one he had been changing.

Disability coverage he added last, and it was the decision he had been avoiding longest. His earning capacity was his largest asset—potentially worth more than a million dollars across his remaining working years. Disability that stopped him from working would eliminate that asset instantly while his expenses continued. He chose own-occupation coverage, which pays when you can't perform your specific job, not just any job. About $90 monthly.

Umbrella liability coverage extended protection beyond his auto and renter's policy limits—one million dollars of additional coverage for about $15 monthly. Judgments can target future earnings, not just current assets. The umbrella protects both.

His total monthly protection: approximately $220.

That $220 shields against losses that would require years to rebuild.

Two rules governed the calibration. As a general planning principle, many people review whether liability coverage is sufficient relative to their assets and future earnings, because minimum legal limits may not provide enough protection in a serious claim. Property coverage should reflect replacement cost, not original purchase price—construction costs and market values move at different rates, and the gap matters when you file a claim.

The Decisions He Couldn't Leave Open

Insurance protects against events. Documents protect against decisions—the ones you can't make because you're incapacitated, or the ones that happen after you're gone.

Evan established four:

A will specifies how assets are distributed after death. Without one, local law decides—often in ways that conflict with what the person would have chosen. Probate for undocumented estates can consume significant time and cost, depending on the estate and jurisdiction. Evan's will specifies asset distribution, names an executor, and designates guardians for future children.

A durable power of attorney authorizes someone to make financial decisions if he is incapacitated. Without it, family members may need to seek court authority for financial decisions—often an expensive, slow, and invasive process at the worst possible moment.

A healthcare power of attorney and living will authorize someone to make medical decisions if he can't and specify preferences for end-of-life care. These can reduce confusion and lower the risk of family disputes during medical crises.

Beneficiary designations name recipients for retirement accounts, life insurance, and bank accounts with payable-on-death designations. These assets bypass probate entirely—but only if the designations are current. In many cases, they can override instructions in a will, which is why keeping them current matters. An outdated beneficiary designation sends assets to the wrong person regardless of what the will says.

Evan established all four through an online legal service for a few hundred dollars. That small cost can prevent potential probate and guardianship complications worth tens of thousands.

I operated without any of these documents until my late thirties. When I finally established a will and power of attorney, the attorney asked who should make medical decisions if I were incapacitated. I hadn't considered the question. Without designation, local law may assign that authority to family members in a specific order. I realized I had never thought about whether that order matched my preferences—or whether the people at the top of the list knew my values well enough to make those decisions. The documents answered questions I hadn't known to ask.

Where Protection Fails Quietly

The failure that caused Evan's loss was small.

A payment method wasn't updated. The system appeared active. It wasn't.

Protection fails in quiet ways. A policy lapses. A coverage limit becomes outdated as assets grow. A beneficiary designation names someone whose relationship has changed. A document remains unchanged while the circumstances it was written for no longer exist.

This is another version of the Smart Struggle Loop, but quieter. Nothing feels urgent, so the mind postpones the decision. The policy looks active enough. The document looks current enough. The beneficiary designation looks like something to handle later. Protection doesn't usually fail because of one dramatic mistake. It fails because avoidance becomes invisible when nothing is demanding attention. The Loop doesn't always look like panic or overanalysis. Sometimes it looks like silence.

Nothing signals the problem. Until something triggers it.

That is the nature of protection. It is only tested when it is needed. By then, it is too late to build.

The Review That Keeps It Current

After rebuilding, Evan added one rule.

The system had to continue working without constant attention.

Payments were automated to stable accounts. Policies were set at appropriate limits, then left alone between reviews. He chose a specific month—January—for an annual audit: Verify all policies are active, check coverage limits against current assets and income, update beneficiary designations if anything had changed.

He added a quarterly check—fifteen minutes—to confirm automated payments were still processing correctly. That small verification catches the administrative problem before it becomes a coverage gap.

He also built a transition trigger list: marriage, divorce, home purchase, a child, a job change, a significant inheritance. Any of these events requires a protection review, because the circumstances the original documents were written for may no longer apply.

Not constant vigilance. Periodic confirmation that what was built is still running.

The goal was continuity. Because failure doesn't announce itself in advance.

Growth Is Gradual, Loss Is Immediate

Building wealth without protecting it creates an asymmetry.

Growth is gradual. Loss is immediate.

Without protection, a single event can undo years of accumulation. With protection, the same event becomes a contained interruption.

Protection doesn't depend on everything going right. It is built to survive when something goes wrong.

What Remains Unprotected

External safeguards protect assets. They don't protect decisions.

Insurance covers loss after an event. It doesn't prevent the action that creates the loss. Legal structures define outcomes. They don't stop a moment of pressure from bypassing them.

Some risks don't come from events. They come from reactions. Urgency. Pressure. Confusion. Moments where normal caution is replaced by speed.

These are not external failures. They happen inside the decision itself.

The Other Half of Protection

External protection handles predictable risks. Internal awareness handles unpredictable moments.

One protects what you have built. The other protects how you act when something challenges it.

Both are required. Neither replaces the other.

External protections guard your accounts. Internal signals guard your decisions.

Protection is not vigilance. It is what remains in place when vigilance fails.

Chapter 13: The Pressure Someone Else Creates

The Message That Looked Real

Chapter 12 protected your assets from events. A flood, a disability, a legal dispute—these are things that happen to your money. This chapter protects something different: your decisions. Not what you have, but how you act when someone is deliberately trying to move you faster than your judgment can follow.

Chapter 14 will address the internal stress that financial life generates even when systems are working. Here, the threat has a source. Someone is trying to create urgency. And that changes everything about how you recognize it.

The email looked perfect. Subject line: "Urgent: Verify Your Account Within 24 Hours." It looked legitimate—Diane's bank logo, perfectly formatted. It even included her account number, last four digits only, just like real notices. She'd been so careful with her automated debt payments. She checked her dashboard weekly. She followed the systems from earlier chapters.

Her hand moved toward the "Verify Now" button. Then her chest tightened. Not panic—recognition. She recognized the pressure to act immediately. The manufactured urgency. The way her breathing had shortened without her noticing. She paused.

Diane opened her banking app directly (not through the email link), logged in, checked for alerts. Nothing. She called the number on the back of her card. "We didn't send that email," the representative confirmed. "You just avoided a sophisticated phishing attempt."

The tight chest had been her early warning signal. Her body knew before her mind caught up.

Before Analysis Begins

You've built external protection through Chapter 12—insurance, legal documents, account security. Those safeguards create shields around your money. This chapter builds internal recognition—the ability to detect manipulation through body signals before rational analysis even begins.

External defense protects your accounts. Internal recognition protects your decision-making under pressure.

Your leader identity from Chapter 5 taught you that leadership means trusting systems while honoring instinct. In cash flow, that meant building visibility. In debt elimination, it meant automation over willpower. In protection, leadership means recognizing that the greatest defense isn't constant vigilance that creates exhaustion. It's confidence in your ability to pause, verify, and decide from clarity rather than pressure.

Your Body Knows First

Remember your body awareness work from Chapter 3? You learned that your nervous system carries financial memory—tightness, freeze responses, urgency patterns coded from past experiences. Those weren't problems to fix. They were information to read.

This chapter builds on that foundation. Where Chapter 3 helped you recognize how past experiences create present reactions, this chapter treats those reactions as early warning signals. Your body does not only carry memories of past financial stress. It may also register pressure, urgency, or discomfort before your conscious mind has fully processed what is happening.

This is the progression from awareness to protection. You're not managing anxiety. You're using your nervous system's sophisticated threat detection as part of your leader identity.

Robert had eliminated $18,000 in debt over eight months using systematic acceleration. He felt financially confident for the first time in years. Then came the call.

"This is Agent Martinez from the Social Security Administration," the voice said, professional and measured. "Your Social Security number has been compromised in a data breach. We need to verify your information immediately to protect your benefits."

The caller knew Robert's full name, address, and recent debt payment amounts. Robert found himself opening his banking app before his rational mind engaged. The pattern here is precise: Analysis that normally protects him froze under manufactured authority pressure, flipping into compliance instead of verification.

He spent the rest of that day replaying the call, analyzing every moment he should have recognized the red flags. The caller's overly formal tone. The immediate demand for information. The specific knowledge of his debt payments.

"I felt stupid," Robert admits. "Like all the work I'd done to get financially stable was just luck, and I was still the same person who'd gotten into debt in the first place. One phone call exposed me as a fraud."

This emotional spiral is exactly what manipulators count on. Shame keeps victims silent, preventing them from reporting scams or warning others.

This isn't personal failure. It's sophisticated exploitation of how all human brains respond to pressure.

Financial fraud has increased dramatically in recent years. In the United States alone, consumers reported losing about $16 billion to fraud in 2025.[1] Globally, total losses are likely far higher when unreported incidents are included. Most incidents do not rely on sophisticated technical hacking. They rely on manipulation—pressuring people to act before they can verify.

Robert's body registered the signal almost immediately: tight chest, rapid breathing. He paused, hung up, and verified the request through official channels using independently sourced contact information. Once he confirmed the call was fraudulent, he reported it. The pause worked exactly as intended.

"What I realized," Robert explains, "is that the manipulation attempt didn't undo my progress. My response to it demonstrated my progress. The old Robert would have reacted immediately to author-

1. Federal Trade Commission, "FTC Testifies before the Joint Economic Committee on the Agency's Efforts to Combat Fraud," March 25, 2026.

ity pressure. The new Robert recognized the body signal and paused. That's leadership."

Notice what happens in your body when you imagine an unexpected call claiming your financial accounts are compromised. Chest tightness? Shallow breathing? Racing thoughts? That physical response is data, not weakness. Your nervous system is preparing you to act. The question is whether that action serves you or the manipulator.

The Signal Before the Story

Your nervous system often flags pressure before your conscious mind can name it — but the pause it creates, not the sensation itself, is what protects you.

Physical signals serve as early warnings, appearing when financial pressure or deception is present.

Learning to read these signals turns pressure into something you can verify instead of obey. You're not watching for danger constantly—you're trusting your body to alert you when something requires verification.

Your nervous system processes threats faster than conscious thought. When you encounter manipulation, your body responds to patterns (tone of voice, pacing of demands, emotional pressure) within milliseconds. Your conscious mind needs seconds or minutes to analyze the same information.

This isn't a flaw in your thinking. Financial scammers deliberately bypass your rational thinking by creating artificial urgency. They trigger immediate physical responses: urgency, excitement, fear, obligation. Once your body is in threat response, you're more likely to act without verification.

By learning to read your physical responses as information rather than reacting to them immediately, you reclaim the pause between stimulus and response. That pause is where verification lives.

When Pressure Comes From Outside

You already know what to do when your body sends a signal. The RESET process from Chapter 2 applies here because the structure is the same: A trigger arrives, a physical response begins, and the question is whether you will let that response complete automatically or introduce a gap before it does.

With unexpected financial contact, the trigger is external rather than internal—a call, an email, a pitch—but the body's response follows the same architecture. Recognize that something has activated. Exhale before responding. Separate the story the contact is building—"your account is at risk," "this window closes tonight"—from what is actually verifiable. Evaluate through channels you find independently, not the ones you were given. Then act—or don't—from clarity rather than from whatever urgency the contact was designed to produce.

The difference between Chapter 2 and this moment is that here, the pressure has a source that wants something from you.

The Body's Warning Signs

Your body doesn't wait for your conscious mind to confirm a threat. It signals one first.

You have already practiced reading those signals in Chapter 3—learning to distinguish the chest tightness that means "old pattern activating" from the genuine present-moment calm your nervous system is also capable of. The same reading applies here, but now the signal is pointing outward rather than inward.

A tight chest or shallow breathing during unexpected contact may mean your nervous system has caught urgency before you have. The useful move is naming it, even just to yourself: I never make financial decisions during unexpected contacts. I verify independently first.

Gut flutter—the excited sensation that makes one opportunity feel different from all the others—is worth pausing over because that sensation can make caution harder to access. The question that cuts through it is simple: Why does this require a decision right now, and what happens if I take forty-eight hours to research it?

Tension behind the eyes often marks the moment an explanation is outrunning your ability to verify it. The honest response is to ask for exactly what you would need to check it yourself: credentials, documentation, something in writing.

Jaw clenching tends to signal relational pressure—someone leaning on loyalty, guilt, or obligation to move you faster than you would move on your own. The boundary that interrupts it does not need to be elaborate: I need time to consider this without pressure.

And the particular freeze that settles into your shoulders when something feels too complex to follow may be confusion doing its warning work. Legitimate offers can be explained simply, so ask for that simplicity directly.

None of these signals are definitive on their own. All of them are worth a pause. Knowing which one shows up most for you is not weakness—it is the kind of self-awareness that speeds up recognition. One client who had identified her own pattern as gut flutter around opportunity put it this way: "Now when I feel that flutter, it's my cue to pause and ask: 'Why the urgency?' That one question has protected me from three different investment scams this year. The flutter isn't a problem—it's information."

The Rule That Creates the Pause

Robert's recognition worked because he had built verification habits before he needed them. When the body signal appeared, he knew exactly what to do.

Here's how you might build similar habits: You could create a simple rule—"I never make financial decisions during unexpected contacts." This removes the decision from the moment. When unexpected contact occurs, your response is automatic: Pause, verify independently, then decide.

Independent verification means contacting the claimed institution through information you find yourself, not through contact details provided by the unexpected caller or email. If someone claims to be from your bank, you hang up and call the number on your card. If an email claims to be from a company, you navigate to their website directly rather than clicking links in the email.

You might practice this response: "I appreciate the information. I'll verify this through official channels and follow up if needed." Then end the contact. This works for phone calls, emails, text messages, even in-person pressure.

The point of any of this is not to become suspicious of every message, call, or opportunity that arrives unannounced. That would only trade one kind of pressure for another. The point is simpler: notice the signal, pause long enough to verify, and let the outcome do the teaching. That is how protection stays calm instead of becoming its own kind of fear.

Diane nearly invested $15,000 in what looked like a legitimate cryptocurrency platform. Everything appeared professional—slick website, testimonials, "verified" badges. But when she felt the gut flutter (excitement overriding caution), she paused. She researched the company name plus "scam" and found multiple complaints. The gut flutter had warned her. She trusted the signal, verified independently, discovered manipulation, and avoided loss.

What the Near Miss Proved

Even with strong recognition, manipulation attempts will reach you. Scammers are sophisticated and persistent. When this happens, how you process the experience matters as much as how you responded in the moment.

When manipulation attempts occur (and they will), you might move through three emotional beats to maintain confidence:

Recognition: "I encountered manipulation. This is common and not evidence of personal failure. Smart people get targeted precisely because they have resources worth stealing."

Release: "I spotted it before it cost me. My body signals worked. My verification process worked. I've already reported it to help protect others."

Re-centering: "I trust my ability to recognize the signal. I can spot body signals and pause before reacting. This experience demonstrates my capability, not my vulnerability."

Together, these three beats help restore confidence after a near miss: notice the reality (recognition), name it without judgment (release), and normalize the experience as part of systematic life (re-centering).

What Protection Makes Possible

You've learned to recognize manipulation and restore confidence through successful pause-and-verify cycles. Together, those capacities create the foundation for the next question: What do you want this protected life to become?

You've spent Part Three building systematic financial protection—visibility through cash flow management, investing, debt reduction, and external protection. Chapter 13 adds internal recognition: trusting your body's signals to detect manipulation before rational analysis begins.

There's a profound difference between having financial systems and living as someone whose financial systems run automatically while you focus on what matters most.

You built the infrastructure of financial security. That infrastructure was necessary. But infrastructure alone doesn't create meaning. Now that money is handled more systematically, a different question becomes possible: What do you actually want your life to be about? When protection feels more automatic and less effortful, what becomes possible?

You can't design a rich life if your nervous system remains on constant alert. The systems create the foundation. Internal recognition creates the confidence. Together, they create the freedom to ask bigger questions than "How do I protect what I have?"

Financial calm isn't the absence of manipulation attempts. Financial calm is confidence in your ability to recognize and respond to pressure without it undermining your progress. That confidence is what makes design possible.

The Signal Was a Question

You've learned to save, invest, and protect. You've built systems that function without constant oversight. You've automated the mechanics of financial security. Now your task changes—from defending money to directing it.

The tight chest Diane felt wasn't anxiety to eliminate. It was information to read. That signal, and her pause in response to it, protected months of automated savings discipline. But more importantly, it demonstrated something profound: She could trust herself under pressure. That trust is the foundation for everything that follows.

When you no longer fear losing money, you start creating meaning with it. When manipulation attempts become demonstrations of your recognition system working effectively rather than threats to your security, financial decisions feel different. Calmer. More grounded. Less reactive.

Safety isn't the absence of risk. It's confidence in your response.

This confidence is the foundation for Part Four. When you trust yourself to verify independently and recover from near misses, money becomes a tool for designing life. It stops being a threat requiring constant defense.

Once confidence replaces fear, values become your compass. The protection you've built doesn't just defend what you have. It creates space to ask what you want.

In Part Four, you'll design a life money serves—not the other way around. You'll define what rich actually means on your terms. You will build margin for what matters most. You will sustain progress through intentional design that serves your values.

A useful practice here is simple: Identify your primary body signal. The next time unexpected financial contact occurs, notice it, pause, and verify independently before taking any action. If you want to track it, keep the note simple: body signal, verification step, outcome.

This single practice—recognizing your body signal and pausing before responding—builds the trust that makes all other financial decisions feel calmer and more grounded. When you trust your recognition system, you stop second-guessing every unexpected contact. Financial confidence becomes your default state.

Your smartest financial system isn't your budget spreadsheet or investment account. It's your own nervous system—when you learn to read its signals, trust its warnings, and act from clarity rather than pressure.

This habit becomes the micro-skill that Part Four builds on.

With your recognition system in place, you now have the internal safety required to design a life that aligns with your values.

Diane made tea after she hung up with the bank representative. Not to calm herself down—she was already calm.

The tightness in her chest had done its job. She had paused, verified, confirmed. The entire sequence had taken eleven minutes.

She drank the tea and returned to what she had been doing before the email arrived.

That was the entire event.

The signal was never anxiety. It was a question. Most people never stop long enough to hear it.

Interlude: What the Systems Were For

There is a particular kind of quiet that arrives when money stops being an emergency. Not silence. Not the absence of problems. Just the absence of the constant low-level alarm that had been running so long you'd stopped hearing it as alarm and started hearing it as normal.

I remember the first Saturday morning it happened for me. The transfers had run. The bills had paid. The accounts were where they were supposed to be. I had checked—once, the night before—and then I hadn't checked again.

I made coffee. I sat at the table. My wife was reading. My daughter was still asleep.

Nothing needed me.

That sounds small. It wasn't.

For years, something had always needed me on Saturday mornings. Not dramatically. Not a crisis. Just the ambient pull of accounts to review, transfers to verify, decisions to defer. The presence of money as an unfinished task.

That Saturday it was finished. Not perfectly. The system wasn't complete. But it was working.

And working was enough to change the texture of a morning.

This is what the systems were for. Not the spreadsheets. A morning that belonged to you.

PART FOUR: LIVING

The practical work has done what it was supposed to do.

Now the question is no longer how to stabilize money, but how to live inside a life that money no longer runs.

Chapter 14: The Alarm Goes Quiet

Financial calm doesn't begin when the numbers improve. It begins when the morning stops starting with alarm.

Sarah's morning ritual used to begin with dread. Before her feet touched the floor, she was already calculating: rent due in six days, the credit card minimum, whether she could skip lunch to save $12. Her chest tightened before she even checked her phone. By 9 a.m., she had opened her banking app four times, each glance adding another layer of anxiety without changing a single number.

Now she starts differently. Two minutes of intentional breathing before reaching for the phone. A quick review of the spending plan she trusts because she built it herself. The numbers haven't magically improved, but the spiral no longer starts before breakfast.

Calm isn't a function of having more money. It's a function of how your body meets the money you already have.

Sarah, who had been so careful with her systems, was learning something harder now: Good processes don't create calm on their own.

The loop was still there. It just no longer looked like confusion. It looked like checking. Monitoring. Returning to the same numbers for relief and leaving more activated each time.

If Sarah's shift feels impossibly distant given your current stress, that's understandable. The practices in this chapter are tools, not requirements. Your version of financial calm will look different from Sarah's, and that's exactly right.

The Work After Recognition

In Chapter 13, you learned to recognize manipulation through body signals— your nervous system's early warning signal for external threats. Now Chapter 14 extends that body awareness to a different challenge: regulating your own stress response to legitimate financial situations.

Where Chapter 13 taught you to pause and verify before reacting to threats, this chapter teaches you to calm your nervous system so everyday financial decisions don't trigger constant vigilance.

You've built the technical foundation. These systems work. But if checking your account balance still triggers panic, if spending on yourself creates guilt, if financial decisions drain your mental energy—the systems function but you're exhausted. That exhaustion isn't failure. It's what happens when you operate in defensive mode for months or years.

You're entering Part Four with systems stable enough to support the next stage of work. Part Four teaches sustainability—maintaining systems without burning out. This chapter starts that shift by teaching you to regulate the physiological stress response that financial situations trigger.

Your leader identity from Chapter 5 taught you to lead from agency, not reaction. That perspective gave you decision-making authority. But authority without regulation creates exhausted leadership—you're making good decisions while your nervous system stays in threat mode. This chapter adds the missing piece: emotional authority. You're learning to lead from a calm nervous system, not just a capable mind.

Why Money Triggers the Body

Financial stress often shows up in the body before the mind has fully interpreted the situation. Your heart rate may shift when you see a bill. Your breathing may change when you check your account balance. Your shoulders may tense during money conversations. These are not character flaws. They are signs that your nervous system may be responding to perceived threat.

An unexpected bill or low balance can trigger a threat response before you have fully thought through the facts. The body may prepare for danger even when the "danger" is a number on a screen, a due date, or a future uncertainty rather than an immediate physical threat. That mismatch helps explain why financial stress can feel so intense even when the next step is practical and ordinary.[1]

The problem isn't that the body is wrong to care. The problem is that the response can be larger, faster, and more physical than the situation requires. Once you understand that mismatch, the goal becomes less about forcing calm and more about creating enough safety for the next clear action.

---

1. Bruce S. McEwen, "Physiology and Neurobiology of Stress and Adaptation", Physiological Reviews 87, no. 3 (2007): 873–904.

That is why the stress can linger. You can't run from a low balance or fight rising rates, so the body stays activated long after the practical problem has been identified.

Chronic financial stress reliably narrows thinking. Planning shrinks. Perspective collapses. Working memory decreases, future planning becomes harder. Decision-making deteriorates when your nervous system operates in threat mode. The stress that your situation creates makes it harder to think clearly about your situation—a vicious cycle that feels like personal failure but is actually basic biology.

Remember the RESET work from Chapter 2? Your body holds money programming—automatic responses to financial triggers. You learned to recognize patterns. This chapter builds on that recognition: You're learning to work with those responses instead of being carried by them.

I experienced this during a financial crisis—waking at 3 a.m., heart pounding, mentally reviewing numbers I'd already checked a dozen times. The checking helped nothing. Numbers don't change at 3 a.m. But my nervous system couldn't distinguish "financial problem I can't solve right now" from "immediate physical danger."

The solution wasn't thinking different thoughts. It was interrupting the physiological stress response so my brain could function clearly enough to address real problems.

Notice what happens in your body when you imagine an unexpected bill arriving. Chest tightness? Shallow breathing? Racing thoughts? That physical response is data, not weakness. Your nervous system is preparing you to act—you're learning to direct that energy toward clarity rather than panic.

Financial stress isn't a response to your bank balance.

It's a response to what your nervous system believes your bank balance means.

Where Regulation Can Help

Three practices can help. First, recognizing your stress signals before they escalate. Second, applying immediate regulation techniques when stress activates. Third, building sustainable daily practices that reduce how frequently stress activates in the first place.

This approach works well for people who experience chronic financial stress exceeding actual current threat level. It helps those who have some baseline stability, can carve out small amounts of time for self-regulation, and prefer body-based practices.

This approach works best when your nervous system has some baseline capacity—when the primary problem is the Loop itself, not a crisis requiring immediate external support. If you're facing eviction, acute food insecurity, or a mental health emergency, address those first. The analytical mind that built the Loop can also be your greatest ally in accessing the right resources. This chapter will be here when you're ready.

If You Are in Immediate Financial Distress

If you're facing eviction, food insecurity, legal threats, unsafe debt pressure, or a financial emergency that cannot wait, address the crisis first. Do not treat this book as your only support. Contact a qualified financial counselor, legal aid service, social assistance office, crisis support line, or trusted professional in your area. This book can help you recognize patterns, but urgent situations require direct, practical support.

If that situation applies to you, stabilize first. The guidance in this chapter assumes you have enough space to work with your responses, not manage an immediate emergency.

Recognizing Your Stress Signals

Before you can regulate financial stress, you need to catch it early—before it escalates into full panic or shutdown.

Your body gives early warning signs on a spectrum from mild to severe:

Early warning signs might include slight chest tightness when thinking about money, brief urge to check balance "just to be sure," or quick mental calculation of remaining funds.

Escalating signs include persistent chest tightness or shallow breathing, checking accounts four or more times daily, racing thoughts about worst-case scenarios, or avoiding your banking app entirely.

Full activation can include panic when seeing balances, complete avoidance for days or weeks, or physical symptoms like headaches and insomnia.

Learning your personal pattern helps you intervene early. Sarah's signal is chest tightness—when she notices it, she knows to pause and breathe before checking her account. Another common signal is the urge to check your balance "just once more"—when you catch yourself reaching for your phone the third time, use a grounding technique instead.

You might spend this week simply noticing your pattern. When does financial stress appear? What's the first physical signal? How does it escalate? This observation, without trying to change anything yet, builds awareness that makes intervention possible later.

Three Ways to Interrupt the Spiral

When stress activates, you might try one of these three immediate regulation techniques. Each takes ninety seconds to fifteen minutes and interrupts the physiological cascade before it hijacks your thinking.

The Ninety-Second Pause

This is where you return to the Exhale—the physiological pause from the RESET process you learned in Chapter 2—as an immediate interrupt when your body is too activated to think clearly.

When you notice stress signals, you might try this: Exhale fully (count to four). Hold empty lungs briefly (count to two). Inhale slowly through your nose (count to four). Hold (count to two). Repeat three times.

This works because controlled breathing activates your parasympathetic nervous system—the "rest and digest" mode that counteracts fight-or-flight. Ninety seconds of intentional breathing physiologically interrupts the stress response. Once the breath settles, the RESET process becomes available again: Recognize what triggered the response. Separate emotion from data. Evaluate with your adult mind. Take aligned action. You can do this before checking your account, before paying bills, or before money conversations.

Grounding Through the Five Senses

When thought spirals start ("What if I can't pay rent? What if I lose everything?"), you might interrupt them by engaging your senses:

Name five things you see. Four things you can touch. Three things you hear. Two things you smell. One thing you taste.

This works because catastrophic thinking pulls attention into future scenarios. Engaging your senses redirects attention toward what is physically present. Grounding makes it harder for the mind to keep building worst-case scenarios because attention is being redirected toward the present moment.

A Time to Face the Concern

Instead of trying to never think about financial stress, you might contain it to a specific time. Choose fifteen minutes daily or weekly—Sunday morning, Wednesday evening, whatever fits. During that time, you intentionally worry. Review your accounts. Calculate scenarios. List concerns. Write them down. When the fifteen minutes end, you close the notebook and return to other activities.

This works because trying to suppress anxious thoughts typically intensifies them—the more you tell yourself "Don't think about money," the more money dominates your attention. Containment acknowledges the stress while preventing it from consuming your entire day. If anxious thoughts appear outside your containment time, you might tell yourself: "That's a valid concern. I'll address it during Sunday's ritual."

A client tried this and reported: "The first two weeks felt artificial—like I was playing a game with myself. But by week three, my brain started trusting the ritual. When money worries appeared during work, I could genuinely redirect them because I knew Sunday morning was coming. The stress didn't disappear—it just stopped leaking into every moment."

Habits That Make Calm Easier

Short-term techniques interrupt immediate stress. Sustainable practices reduce how frequently stress activates in the first place.

Scheduled Checking

If checking your account triggers anxiety, you might try scheduled checking—same time daily, no "just once more" checks throughout the day. This builds tolerance. The first few times feel uncomfortable. But over weeks, your nervous system learns: "Checking the account at 9 a.m. is safe. I don't need to check again at ten, eleven, one, three, five..."

Values-Based Permission

Financial stress often comes from misalignment between spending and values. You might try this: Before a purchase, ask "Does this serve my top three values?" If yes, the spending carries less guilt. If no, skip it without feeling deprived—you're not restricting yourself, you're choosing alignment.

During a cash flow crisis, I did this check and realized my savings goals were misaligned with immediate reality. My top value: "Get through this intact." That meant redirecting money from long-term savings to immediate stability. Stress remained, but self-judgment stopped.

One Practice at a Time

You might add these practices gradually. Start with one technique for a week—maybe the ninety-second pause before checking accounts. Once that feels automatic, you could add another technique.

One reader tried all the techniques in week one. By day three, they had forgotten which to use when, felt overwhelmed, and quit. Week two, they started over with just the set-time practice. Once that felt automatic, they added the ninety-second pause. Six months later, they used three techniques regularly—but learned them one at a time.

The lesson: Sequential mastery beats simultaneous overwhelm. Start with one. Add more only after the first becomes habit.

When to Seek Professional Support

These practices help with normal financial stress, not clinical anxiety disorders. You might seek licensed mental health care if panic symptoms are recurring, difficult to manage, or interfering with sleep, work, relationships, or daily functioning. Other signs include prolonged sleep disruption, harmful coping behaviors, thoughts of self-harm, or relationship breakdown due to financial stress.

Resources may include community mental health centers, university training clinics, employee assistance programs, public health services, crisis support lines, and online therapy platforms. If cost is a barrier, local community resource lines or social service directories may help connect you with low-cost support in your area.

The First Few Days

If you are ready to try this, you might start simply. For the first day, just observe. Notice when financial stress rises, what seemed to trigger it, and how it shows up in your body. Do not change anything yet. Just observe.

On another day, before checking your account, try the ninety-second pause. Notice whether the intensity changes. After a few days, you might look back and ask: Which signals appeared most often? Which practice helped create even a small amount of space?

This gradual approach respects that you are already managing a lot. You are not adding a complex new system. You are testing one small practice and seeing whether it helps.

The Practice You Return To

You will not use these practices perfectly. You will forget the ninety-second pause and check your account eight times in an hour. You will skip the practice and let worry bleed into your entire Sunday.

That is normal and understandable. The Smart Struggle Loop can even hijack self-regulation, turning helpful practices into another thing you feel you should perfect. These are not habits you master once. They are tools you return to. The goal is not to eliminate financial stress. The goal is to recover more quickly when stress activates.

Last month, an unexpected tax bill arrived. I caught myself checking my account six times before noon, each glance adding anxiety without changing reality. I recognized the spiral: obsessive checking disguised as staying informed. I gave the concern a defined place. Fifteen minutes of dedicated worry, then back to work. The bill did not shrink, but the spiral stopped.

I still have financial stress. When I ran my engineering practice, cash flow uncertainty was constant—receivables delayed, project timelines shifting, quarterly tax obligations appearing without warning. Medical expenses still appear unexpectedly. But recovery time has shortened. What used to pull me into days of anxiety now resolves more quickly because I have trusted practices to interrupt the spiral.

You are not trying to never feel financial stress. You are trying to stop the stress from compounding itself: stress about being stressed, anxiety about being anxious, shame about body responses you cannot fully control.

Your leader perspective from Chapter 5 operates differently now. When you first claimed that perspective, it was about making decisions from agency instead of reaction. Now that same perspective includes how you respond under pressure. You lead your financial life not because stress disappears, but because stress no longer has to make every decision for you.

What Calm Makes Possible

You've learned to calm your nervous system around money triggers. That regulation creates mental space for the next question: What do you actually want your money to do for your life? Not what social media says. Not what cultural scripts dictate. What genuinely matters based on your authentic values.

The real power comes from combining nervous system regulation with intentional life design—building toward something that actually serves you rather than just managing stress about what you have.

Regulation creates space.

What fills it is design.

From Control to Clarity

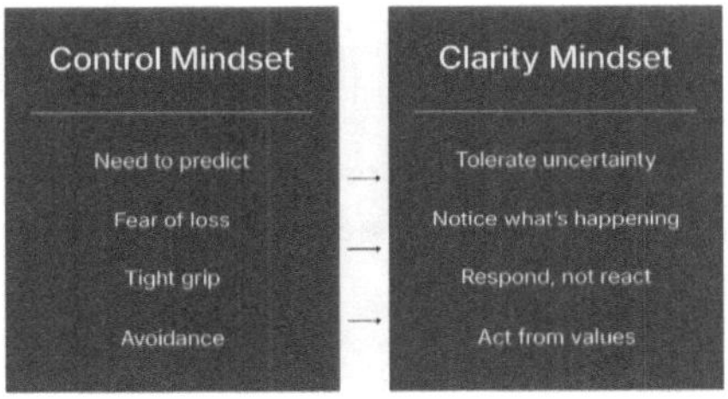

Clarity replaces control, not effort.

Chapter 15: A Life Money Serves

Irene thought she knew what success looked like. The corner office, the luxury car lease, the downtown condo with floor-to-ceiling windows. She'd been chasing that image for eight years, climbing the corporate ladder, earning more each year. On paper, she was winning.

Then her father had a stroke. Three months of flying back and forth to help her mother, missing the career trajectory milestones, watching promotions go to people who could stay late for client dinners. She expected to feel devastated. Instead, she felt relief.

The life she'd been building wasn't the life she actually wanted. The corner office meant nothing if she couldn't leave for family emergencies. The luxury car was just expensive stress. The condo was empty most evenings because work consumed everything else.

She'd been following someone else's script for success, mistaking cultural expectations for personal values.

She had built the version of success she was taught to admire and discovered it offered no relief.

James had the opposite problem. He'd achieved every financial milestone the personal finance community celebrated: six-month emergency fund, maxed retirement accounts, paid-off house. His net worth exceeded most people's lifetime goals. Yet anxiety about money consumed him constantly. Every market dip triggered panic. Every unexpected expense felt like failure. He'd eliminated financial risk but couldn't eliminate financial worry.

Both Irene and James found themselves stuck: Irene chasing someone else's definition of success, James discovering that financial security doesn't automatically create psychological calm. The gap between money and meaning operates in both directions.

If either realization feels familiar, you're not alone. Maybe you're succeeding at someone else's definition of a rich life. Or maybe you've achieved financial milestones that don't deliver the peace you expected.

Many people spend years pursuing goals they inherited rather than chose. The gap between what we think we should want and what we actually value creates a specific kind of exhaustion that no amount of income increase can fix.

A rich life isn't something you perform. It is something you can actually live inside. This chapter is about finding the version of enough that belongs to you, not the one you were taught to admire.

What Makes a Life Rich

A life money serves is not defined by income level or net worth. It is defined by whether your spending, time, and attention are aligned with what matters to you. Someone earning $40,000 annually and living according to their real priorities may have more of what money is supposed to buy than someone earning $400,000 while pursuing values they do not genuinely hold.

Living according to your own values rather than inherited scripts is the version of wealth most likely to satisfy.

The calm you learned in Chapter 14 creates the space to ask a clearer question. When stress is not driving your thinking, you can examine what you value instead of what you think you should value. Under pressure, most people default to safety scripts, cultural expectations, or whatever reduces the immediate threat. Values clarity requires enough calm to tell the difference.

You're entering Part Four with systems steady enough that the question shifts from managing money to directing it with intention.

Design Gives Planning a Direction

Financial planning focuses on mechanics—how much to save, where to invest, when to retire. It answers tactical questions with numbers.

Life design focuses on meaning—what you are building toward, why it matters, and how money serves your real priorities. It answers strategic questions with values.

You have spent the previous chapters building the foundation: steadier income, clearer cash flow, debt structure, protection, and more calm around money itself. Planning creates the foundation. Design determines what you build on that foundation.

Planning asks: "Can I afford this?" Design asks: "Does this serve who I actually am?"

Both matter. But many people skip directly to planning without ever clarifying what they are planning for. They optimize toward someone else's destination. This chapter brings design forward, so your planning serves your values, not inherited scripts.

Values Versus Scripts

Most people confuse values with scripts. A value is something you authentically care about when you examine your actual experience. A script is something you think you should care about because culture, family, or society says it matters.

Scripts sound like these:

"I should own a home by thirty."

"Successful people drive nice cars."

"Real wealth means early retirement."

Values sound like these:

"I feel most alive when I'm creating something new."

"Geographic flexibility matters more to me than owning property."

"I love my work and can't imagine retiring early."

The difference isn't always obvious. Sometimes scripts masquerade as values for years. You might genuinely believe you value homeownership until you examine why. Then you realize it's because everyone told you that's what financial success looks like, not because you actually want the responsibility of maintaining property.

I thought I valued aggressive wealth accumulation until a business crisis forced me to redirect savings toward immediate stability. The relief I felt revealed the truth: I'd been following a script about what "financially responsible people do" rather than honoring my actual value of "get through this intact." The script said I was failing. My values said I was making the right choice.

My definition of success shifted across life stages: early career focus on building a business, then sustainability after burnout, then flexibility when family needed me. None of these contradicted each other—they represent appropriate responses to different circumstances. Your values at twenty-five don't lock you into those same priorities at forty. Staying locked into an early definition means chasing a script that no longer serves who you've become.

Decades of research in Self-Determination Theory, developed by Edward Deci and Richard Ryan, suggest that goals oriented around autonomy, competence, and relatedness tend to support deeper well-being than goals oriented mainly around status or appearance.[1] What seems to matter more than achieving a goal is whether the goal itself reflects authentic values.

What Your Life Already Reveals

Your cash flow system from Chapter 9 already gives you the data you need for values identification. Those weekly reviews showed where money actually flows. Now use that spending data not just for allocation adjustments, but for values revelation. The numbers tell you what you're funding—whether you meant to or not.

A quick diagnostic: Ask yourself, "Where in my life do my actions contradict the values I say matter most?" These contradictions reveal where stress, guilt, or financial friction originates.

James realized his constant monitoring never came from responsibility—it came from trying to avoid feeling unsafe. Once he named "growth" and "health" as true values, money aligned with who he wanted to become, not who he feared he was.

Examine reality:

---

1. Edward L. Deci and Richard M. Ryan, "The 'What' and 'Why' of Goal Pursuits: Human Needs and the Self-Determination of Behavior," Psychological Inquiry 11, no. 4 (2000): 227–268.

Look at your calendar from the past month. Where did your time actually go? Time reveals priorities more honestly than intentions do.

Review your spending from the past three months. What did you actually spend money on? Money often follows priorities, pressures, and scripts before we consciously name them.

Identify moments of satisfaction. When did you feel genuinely content in the past year? Not Instagram-worthy moments—genuine contentment. What needs were being met?

Identify moments of resentment. When did you feel obligated to spend money or time on something that didn't align with what you care about? The resentment points to values conflicts.

From this examination, draft your top three to five values based on where your time, money, and contentment actually go.

William, a software engineer, did this exercise expecting to confirm he valued career achievement. His calendar showed sixty-hour work weeks. His spending showed takeout because he had no time to cook, a gym membership he never used, and weekend purchases trying to compensate for weekday misery. His satisfaction moments? The rare Saturdays he had energy to play guitar, which he hadn't done in months. His resentment? Constant. The exercise revealed a massive gap between the "ambitious tech professional" script he was following and his actual value of "making music with my hands." He'd been so busy climbing a ladder he didn't realize it was leaning against the wrong building.

If one of your core values is family connection, that might mean allocating budget toward shared experiences instead of impulse purchases. If your value is learning, you might shift discretionary spending toward courses rather than gadgets. Values translate into concrete money decisions when you let them guide allocation rather than inherited scripts.

The identity shift you made earlier in this book wasn't just about how you handle money decisions. It extends to who gets to define what a good outcome looks like. You don't just lead your financial decisions—you define what success means in your financial life. That authority is yours, not your parents' definition, not your industry's benchmark, and not the financial content you consume.

If drafting your values feels forced or artificial—like you're writing what sounds good rather than what's true—pause here. Values identification isn't about aspirational statements. It's about recognizing what your actual behavior already reveals. The calendar and spending data are harder to romanticize. Start there, not with who you wish you were.

Where the Gaps Appear

Once you have identified your values, look at how well your current life aligns with them. This is not about judgment. It is about clarity.

For each value, rate current alignment on a 1–10 scale. A "10" means your time and money consistently flow toward this value. A "1" means this value receives almost no resources despite its importance to you.

Irene's alignment assessment revealed stark gaps. Her top value: "being present for family." Her current alignment: 3/10. She spent sixty hours weekly at work, had minimal time for family visits, and felt guilty constantly. Her second value: "health and energy." Current alignment: 4/10. Takeout most nights, irregular sleep, exercise squeezed in between meetings when she remembered.

The gaps weren't failures—they were data. They showed where her life structure conflicted with what actually mattered to her.

James's assessment revealed different gaps. His top value: "financial security." Current alignment: 10/10—he'd systematically built strong protection. But his second value: "enjoying the present moment." Current alignment: 2/10. He'd sacrificed present enjoyment so completely for future security that he couldn't access contentment even after achieving his financial goals.

Notice patterns in your alignment assessment. Maybe certain values consistently receive resources while others get ignored. Maybe some misalignments feel changeable while others feel structural. Both insights matter.

One Small Reallocation

Once you know your values and see current alignment, you can make intentional shifts—small reallocations that increase consistency between what matters and where money goes.

Start small. Don't try to realign your entire life overnight. Choose one value with low alignment and one concrete shift you can make this month.

Irene's first shift: declining one evening meeting weekly to have dinner with family. This required difficult conversations with her manager about boundaries. But it increased her family presence alignment from 3/10 to 5/10—still not perfect, but meaningfully better.

Her second shift: reducing the cost of the luxury car arrangement and redirecting $200 monthly toward a health and energy fund—cooking classes, quality groceries, a standing desk. Small monetary amount, significant values impact.

James's shift looked different. He'd been so focused on accumulating that spending on present enjoyment triggered guilt. His first reallocation: $150 monthly toward intentional joy—concert tickets, weekend trips, experiences he'd been postponing indefinitely. Not large relative to his finances, but meaningful in a different way. He was learning to access the security he'd built instead of just building more.

The Smart Struggle Loop can appear in values work as endless clarification exercises without making actual changes. Once clarity exists, the shift is from analysis to reallocation.

Try small experiments. Redirect money from one category to another for a month. Notice how it feels. Does the shift increase alignment? Does it reduce resentment? Use the data to inform your next shift.

When Values Change

Your rich life at twenty-five might be adventure and flexibility. At forty with young children: stability and community. At sixty approaching retirement: generosity and legacy. None of these contradict each other—they represent appropriate responses to different life stages.

Evolution doesn't mean you lacked clarity before. It means your priorities shift as life unfolds. Irene wasn't wrong to spend eight years building toward the corner office. That reflected what she understood success to require at twenty-six. Her father's stroke revealed that her priorities had changed. The corner office still matters to some people at thirty-four. It stopped mattering to her. Both positions are valid.

Daniel thought changing his definition meant admitting failure. He'd spent five years building toward early retirement at forty-five—aggressive saving, side hustles, constant optimization. Then his brother died suddenly at forty-two. Daniel realized he'd been so focused on "future freedom" that he'd sacrificed present relationships. He wasn't wrong to pursue early retirement—that goal served him for years. But loss revealed a value shift: Present connection now mattered more than accelerated timeline. Redesigning his rich life didn't mean the previous five years were wasted. It meant his values had evolved, and honoring that evolution was leadership, not failure.

You're allowed to want different things at different life stages. You're allowed to change direction without framing your previous path as a mistake. You're allowed to build toward something, achieve it, discover it doesn't satisfy—and choose something else.

Others' timelines don't set the pace for yours. Someone designing their rich life at twenty-two while you're still figuring out survival at thirty-two isn't ahead. They're on a different path with different circumstances and possibly different starting advantages. Your clarity at forty might be deeper than someone else's at twenty-five because you've tested values against more life experience.

If this entire chapter feels overwhelming—like you're being asked to redesign your whole life when you're just trying to get through this month—that's valid and understandable. Values work happens when you have margin for it. If you're in survival mode, survival itself is the priority right now. You can return to this framework when circumstances shift.

What the Week Reveals

If you are ready to try this, begin with one simple week of observation.

Look at last month's calendar. Notice which activities aligned with your values, which felt neutral, and which conflicted with what matters to you. Then look at three months of spending the same way. Which spending supported the life you say you want? Which spending belonged more to pressure, habit, obligation, or script?

Then look for evidence from the past year. When did you feel genuinely content? What need was being met? When did you spend time or money out of obligation and feel resentment afterward? What value was being crowded out?

From that review, draft three values that appear in your actual life, not just in your ideal self-image. For each one, ask how well your current time and money support it. Then choose one small shift: one amount, one category, one habit, one boundary, one decision.

You are not redesigning your entire life. You are gathering data about the life you are already living.

The calendar is hard to romanticize. So is the spending record. That is both their value and the reason many people avoid looking. You have probably spent more time avoiding one uncomfortable number than this review would require.

You have learned to clarify your values and assess the gap between money and what matters. But clarity does not automatically change behavior, especially around spending. Knowing your top value is family connection does not stop the impulse purchase. Understanding that you are following a luxury-car script does not automatically help you choose differently the next time you are in a dealership.

Clarity and allocation are different capabilities.

Chapter 16: Strategic Spending

Irene knew exactly what mattered to her. After working through Chapter 15's values exercise, she'd identified her top values: being present for family, health and energy, and financial security. She felt clear, even proud of the clarity.

Then she looked at her credit card statement. Two hundred dollars at Target on things she couldn't remember buying. Eighty dollars on restaurant meals she'd eaten alone, scrolling her phone. Another subscription charge for a streaming service she'd forgotten she had. She'd spent zero dollars on art supplies—the thing she claimed brought her joy. Zero dollars toward the emergency fund that would give her the security she said she valued.

She had clear values. Her spending reflected none of them. The gap between knowing what mattered and actually allocating money toward it felt like a canyon she didn't know how to cross.

If you've felt this disconnect—understanding your values but watching your money go everywhere except toward them—you are facing the problem this chapter takes up. Values clarification is the first step. Strategic spending is the second: a way to translate what you care about into where your dollars actually go.

The work now is learning to pause long enough for spending to pass through what matters before it becomes automatic.

You have what this chapter requires: clarity about what matters, and enough calm to act on it. Now the work is building spending systems that turn intention into consistent action.

Why Knowledge Doesn't Change Spending

Knowing what matters doesn't automatically change spending behavior. If you know your top value is family presence but your swipe habit funds status purchases, you don't need a harsher budget. You need rails that make the aligned choice the easy choice.

This disconnect happens for two reasons. First, stress hijacks decision-making. Financial stress reduces cognitive capacity—and when you're running on a threat response, spending defaults to whatever reduces the immediate pressure, not whatever serves your actual values.

Second, cultural scripts override authentic values. The "shoulds" you inherited masquerade as personal priorities until you examine them directly. Without a system that explicitly channels money toward what matters to you, spending defaults to whatever calms the moment or satisfies the loudest script.

Many budgets do not solve this because they rely too heavily on willpower and restriction, which can increase stress and activate script-following. You need a system that does not depend on perfect calm in the moment, but creates structure that makes values-aligned spending the easier path.

Why Budgets Collapse for Smart People

Many people assume the gap between values and spending is a willpower problem. That assumption is often wrong. The gap often widens because many budgeting systems operate through restriction, guilt, and constant self-monitoring.

Budgets collapse for three reasons that have nothing to do with your character:

First, they operate on deprivation. You identify spending categories, set limits based on what you "should" spend, and try not to exceed them. Every purchase becomes a test of worthiness. The shame creates stress, and stress reduces cognitive capacity for good decision-making.

Second, they're static in a dynamic life. You set January's budget based on normal circumstances. Then your car breaks down in February, your kid needs unexpected school supplies in March, you get invited to a wedding in April. Traditional budgets treat these as failures, but they're not failures—they're life.

Third, they focus on restriction rather than direction. Traditional budgets tell you what not to spend. Strategic spending tells you what to prioritize. People sustain approach behaviors—moving toward values—more consistently than avoidance behaviors like restricting temptation.

I spent years failing at budgets before I realized the problem wasn't me, it was the tool. I'd set reasonable limits, track diligently for three weeks, then something unexpected would happen. The budget would break, I'd feel like I'd failed, I'd abandon tracking entirely for months. The budget structure itself created the failure cycle.

The anxiety about not having a perfect budget led to rigid rules, which inevitably broke, triggering more anxiety and system abandonment. The cycle kept me swinging between overcontrol and no control.

One particularly brutal month, I exceeded my budget in six different categories through normal life happening. I sat staring at my spreadsheet feeling like a financial disaster, while the actual damage was maybe two hundred dollars I could easily absorb. The emotional toll of perceived failure far exceeded the actual financial impact. That's when I realized: A system that makes you feel like a failure for living normally isn't helping you.

If you're thinking, "But I've tried budgets and I AM the problem, I lack discipline," that's understandable. But traditional budget failure isn't evidence of weak character. It's evidence that the tool doesn't match how humans actually make decisions under stress. You're not broken. The system you were using may not have matched how you actually make decisions under stress.

Traditional budgets fail because they assume you're making decisions from a calm, rational state. Most people aren't. The approach in this chapter starts from where you actually are—and builds the structure around that reality, not around an idealized version of who you should be when you open a spreadsheet.

The Four Places Money Flows

Instead of restrictive categories with spending limits, use four categories that channel money toward values-aligned purposes. Think of them as rivers, not buckets. Money flows through them dynamically rather than getting trapped in fixed monthly containers.

Your cash flow tracking already shows how money moves through your accounts. Strategic spending uses that same information but reads it differently. You're no longer just observing flow—income arriving, money allocated, spending happening. You're asking a different question: Does this flow serve what actually matters to you?

If these four categories feel overwhelming, like you're being asked to track four separate systems, pause here. You're not adding complexity. You're naming what's already happening. Your money already flows to essentials, growth, joy, and irregular expenses. These categories make that flow visible—and intentional.

The power of this framework isn't in the categories themselves—it's in giving you language to make conscious trade-offs. When you know exactly what you're choosing between, spending decisions become clearer.

Essentials: Stability First

Purpose: Cover non-negotiable survival and stability needs.

Includes: Housing, utilities, basic food, transportation to work, minimum debt payments, essential insurance, childcare if you work.

Doesn't include: Upgraded versions. Essentials means safe, workable housing, not the dream version. Reliable transportation, not a luxury vehicle.

Allocation: This category gets first priority. Calculate actual monthly essentials cost. That amount is non-negotiable before anything else.

Why it matters: You can't build a values-aligned life without stability. When you've covered essentials, you can make intentional choices with remaining money.

Daniel calculated his essentials at $2,800 monthly: rent, utilities, groceries, car payment, insurance, minimum student loan payment. That clarity let him negotiate the four-day work week. He knew exactly what baseline he needed to maintain.

Growth: Future Capacity

Purpose: Build financial capacity that expands future options.

Includes: Emergency fund contributions, debt payoff beyond minimums, retirement savings, skill development that increases earning potential.

Allocation: After essentials, aim for 10–20% of income. If that's impossible, start with 1–5%. The percentage matters less than the consistency.

Why it matters: Values-aligned living isn't just about present spending. It's about building the financial capacity to maintain alignment long-term. An emergency fund means unexpected expenses don't force you off your values path.

Irene, from Chapter 15, redirected her growth spending dramatically. She'd been saving aggressively for a house down payment while feeling constant pressure to work overtime. After her father's stroke clarified that family presence mattered more than homeownership, she made a values-aligned shift. She cut her down payment savings by 75%, redirected that money toward building an emergency fund that would let her take unpaid family leave without financial crisis. Same growth category, different strategic purpose serving her actual values.

The trade-off: A higher growth allocation (15–25%) may build future capacity faster and create a larger security buffer—but it can also mean more present-life restriction and postponed experiences. A lower growth allocation (0–10%) may allow more present-life satisfaction and experiences now—but it usually means slower wealth building and a smaller security buffer.

Neither is wrong. The choice should be intentional based on your actual values from Chapter 15, not automatic because financial advice says you "should" save aggressively.

Joy: Chosen Spending

Purpose: Fund life spending that genuinely serves your authentic values.

Includes: Whatever actually brings you satisfaction aligned with your Chapter 15 values. Daily coffee if that genuinely matters. Art supplies if creativity is your value. Travel if adventure is your value.

Doesn't include: Spending that's scripted rather than valued. If you're buying things because "successful people have them" rather than because they genuinely improve your life, that's not joy—that's performance.

Allocation: After essentials and growth, whatever remains splits between joy and the flexible buffer.

Irene, from the opening story, realized her Target spending wasn't joy—it was stress relief shopping that left her feeling worse afterward. Her actual joy spending: art classes ($80 monthly), supplies ($40), weekend coffee while sketching ($60). Total: $180 monthly. Less than the Target habit cost, but aligned with her actual values. The shift from reactive to intentional spending didn't require earning more money—it required clarity about what joy actually meant to her.

Flexible Buffer: Life Happens Fund

Purpose: Absorb irregular expenses without destroying your system.

Includes: Car repairs, medical co-pays, birthday gifts, wedding invitations, holiday travel, annual fees, anything that doesn't happen monthly but does happen predictably over time.

Allocation: Aim for 10–15% of income. Build this buffer until it reaches one to two months of essentials, then maintain it there.

Why it matters: Life's irregular expenses aren't emergencies—they're predictable unpredictability. The flexible buffer prevents normal life from feeling like constant crisis.

This category is where most traditional budgets fail. They treat irregular expenses as budget failures rather than as a category that needs dedicated funding. When you fund the buffer proactively, car repairs don't trigger guilt or panic—they're what the buffer exists for.

A Rhythm You Can Keep

Your cash flow reviews from Chapter 9 give you the data foundation. Adapt those weekly reviews to include values interpretation:

Weekly: Check spending against your four categories. Notice where money actually went. Adjust next week's intentions if needed.

Monthly: Estimate alignment. Are your categories roughly aligned with your targets? If not, what shifted and why?

Quarterly: Re-read your top values from Chapter 15. Are they still accurate? Review your joy category spending. Is it still funding what actually matters?

Strategic allocation can become anxious micromanagement. If you find yourself spending more time tracking categories than living your values, the system has replaced the purpose. That is the moment to simplify.

Daniel tried tracking every purchase to the penny, color-coding spreadsheets, calculating daily category balances. Three weeks in, he burned out completely. Month two, he tried once-weekly reviews that took ten minutes. That rhythm stuck. The insight: The rhythm should feel lighter than avoidance, not heavier than the problem it was meant to solve.

When Life Limits Your Options

This approach assumes income exceeds survival costs with some margin for choice. Not everyone has that.

If your income barely covers essentials: You're not failing at strategic spending. You're managing survival. The system becomes relevant when circumstances provide margin.

If debt payments consume most non-essential income: Growth temporarily becomes debt elimination. Same principle—building future capacity—but the mechanism is reducing obligation rather than accumulating assets.

If you have variable income: Use this waterfall on every paycheck. Priority order: (1) Essentials floor, (2) Growth floor (even if tiny), (3) Joy (percentage of whatever came in), (4) Buffer fill.

If you're supporting family beyond your household: Their essentials become part of your essentials category.

If health or disability costs consume disproportionate income—medical expenses, adaptive equipment, therapy, medications—these belong in essentials even when they're catastrophically expensive.

These constraints aren't personal failings. They're structural realities affecting what's possible.

Escaping the Comparison Trap

Social media shows everyone else's spending choices without showing their full financial picture. Your 10 percent growth allocation at $40,000 income might represent more discipline than someone's 30 percent allocation at $200,000 income.

The only meaningful comparison is you now versus you six months ago. Are your spending choices slightly more aligned with your stated values than they were? That's progress.

The Three-Question Spending Filter

Before reaching for your wallet, use the pause you have already practiced. That gap is where the aligned choice lives.

When facing a spending decision—especially in the joy category where values show up most clearly—use this simple filter:

Question 1: "Does this align with one of my top three values?" If not, the answer is usually no unless it's maintenance spending that keeps life functioning.

Question 2: "Is this the best way to honor that value right now?" Sometimes saying yes to one values-aligned expense means saying no to another. A concert ticket honors "creative experiences," but if you've already spent this month's joy allocation on art supplies that also honor that value, this might wait.

Question 3: "Can I afford this without disrupting my growth or essentials?" Even perfectly aligned spending becomes problematic if it compromises baseline security.

This filter takes about ten seconds. It doesn't require a budget spreadsheet or category lookup. It just asks: Does this spending serve my actual life design or am I following a script?

Many people abandon their spending plans not because they lack discipline, but because reactive spending takes over when stress hits.

The pause-and-filter approach creates space between trigger and action.

When Spending Becomes Shared

But you don't spend money in isolation. Every joy decision happens in social context: invitations from friends who earn more than you, expectations from family who prioritize differently, community needs that genuinely matter to you.

The spending filter works well for solo decisions. Making it work in relationship requires different skills.

Values-aligned spending isn't discipline. It is the removal of a conflict that was never yours to resolve.

Interlude: The Part You Cannot Automate

Everything so far has been yours to decide—your accounts, your allocations, your debt plan, your systems, your values. All of it answerable by you.

Chapter 17 changes that.

The people in your life didn't read this book. They carry their own money stories, shaped by pressures, fears, and experiences that aren't yours. Some of those stories will align with the life you're building. Most will not.

You cannot automate this tension. You cannot systematize it. You cannot reduce it to a clean set of rules.

What you can do is quieter, and harder: See it clearly, and stay yourself inside it anyway.

I spent years trying to resolve it cleanly—family expectations, professional signals, social norms that never quite matched the life I was building. None of it resolved cleanly. Some of it still hasn't.

But I stopped expecting it to. I stopped treating the tension as failure.

The systems could handle what they could handle. The rest required something else.

Not another system.

A posture.

Chapter 17: Money in Community

Andrew started avoiding dinner with his college friends. Not consciously at first—just convenient excuses. Too tired. Work project. Feeling off. The truth emerged slowly: He couldn't handle another evening listening to them casually discuss their stock portfolios, vacation home purchases, and six-figure bonuses. Meanwhile, he was still digging out of student debt at thirty-four.

His silence about his financial reality created distance. Their assumptions about his situation—that everyone in their circle had similar resources—made every gathering feel like performance. He'd learned to deflect questions about why he wasn't buying property, why he still had roommates, why he couldn't join the ski trip.

When he finally mentioned his debt situation to one friend over coffee, expecting judgment, the response shocked him: "I've been carrying $80,000 in loans for six years. I just never mention it because everyone seems so successful."

Your money life doesn't exist in isolation. It develops in relationship with the people around you—family, friends, partners, colleagues, online communities. These relationships shape what you believe is possible, what feels normal, and what community celebrates. Some relationships support your financial transformation. Others undermine it, often unintentionally.

This chapter teaches you how to navigate money in relationships without betraying your values or damaging your connections. You'll learn to set boundaries kindly, practice generosity that fits your capacity, and build a community that supports rather than undermines your financial health.

You've built the foundation—nervous system calm, values clarity, and strategic spending systems. Now you face the hardest part: maintaining those systems when other people are involved.

Most people unconsciously match the financial behaviors of the groups around them, often without realizing their choices were shaped by social norms rather than personal values. Andrew's isolation wasn't unusual—when everyone around you appears financially successful, admitting struggle feels like admitting failure. But that appearance is often performance, not reality. It is easy to overestimate others' financial stability while hiding your own challenges, creating the illusion that everyone else has it figured out.

Why Money Is Never Individual

Everything you've built—the nervous system regulation, the values clarity, the spending systems—exists inside a social context that either holds it in place or quietly pulls it apart. None of it operates in isolation.

Your community context either supports those changes or undermines them. The calmest nervous system, clearest values, and most strategic spending will struggle if your social environment constantly pulls you away from your goals. This chapter addresses how to design community support that sustains everything you've built.

Three Layers of Money Community

Your social environment operates across three layers, each serving different functions.

Layer One: Inner Circle

The first layer is your inner circle—intimate relationships. This includes romantic partners, immediate family, very close friends, and people whose financial reality intersects with yours or whose opinions significantly affect your wellbeing.

This layer has the most power to support or undermine transformation. A partner who does not share your debt payoff urgency creates constant negotiation. A parent who treats your financial independence as rejection generates guilt. A close friend who mocks your restraint makes every values-aligned choice feel like sacrifice.

What you need here, at minimum, is respect for your choices even if others would not make the same ones. Ideally, you have active support: adjusted spending, progress celebration, patience with constraints, and room for honest conversations.

Daniel, from Chapter 16, kept his four-day work week decision private from his father for six months, deflecting questions about "getting serious." When he finally explained his values directly—creative expression mattered more than maximum income—his father's response was not full acceptance. But the explicit conversation changed the dynamic. It moved the tension from assumed disappointment to acknowledged difference.

Remember your leader identity from Chapter 5? Community context tests that perspective. When everyone around you treats certain spending as mandatory, claiming authority over your financial choices requires social courage, not just internal conviction. The RESET process from Chapter 2 works differently in community. You are interrupting not just your own triggers, but the triggers created by social pressure. That is harder.

If this resonates—if you are navigating family expectations that conflict with your financial choices—explicit conversation does not always create harmony. But it often reduces the invisible weight of unspoken disappointment.

Layer Two: Support Network

The second layer is your support network—chosen community. This includes mentors, peer groups, online forums, accountability circles, and people you interact with regularly around shared goals but whose lives do not directly intersect with yours financially.

This layer provides modeling, accountability, and normalization. When you are surrounded by people pursuing similar goals, required behaviors feel normal rather than extreme.

What you need here is people at different stages of the journey. Too many beginners and you may lack success models. Too many advanced practitioners and everything can feel unattainably distant.

I have witnessed how powerful peer support can be for financial transformation. A colleague in his thirties found his debt payoff community through a Reddit forum when he had $85,000 in education debt. The anonymity let him be transparent in ways he could not be with colleagues, where admitting debt felt like admitting failure. Watching others with larger balances making steady progress made his own situation feel manageable.

Three years later, when he cleared his debt, he stayed active helping newcomers. That reciprocity made the community sustainable. It also showed me how critical peer support can be for maintaining momentum through difficult financial transitions.

Layer Three: Environmental Inputs

The third layer is environmental inputs—the broader cultural context shaping what you absorb through repeated exposure. This includes media consumption, social media feeds, workplace culture, neighborhood norms, financial content, and cultural narratives about what success should look like.

This layer operates through accumulation. One Instagram post showing luxury consumption may not change your spending. Five hundred posts over six months can quietly normalize luxury consumption as the baseline.

The work here is deliberate curation. Unfollow accounts that trigger spending urges. Follow accounts modeling behaviors you are building. Replace financial news designed for anxiety with educational content aligned with your goals.

Irene, from Chapters 15 and 16, realized her Instagram feed normalized lifestyles she could not afford and did not actually want. After systematically unfollowing accounts that triggered comparison, her spending shifted within two months—not through discipline, but through a redesigned environment where consumption messaging decreased.

When Support Has a Cost

When my income grew, the challenges shifted. Family expected I would help with tuition and emergencies—and they were not wrong. Having lived in Singapore, I had seen how common this was: success meant shared responsibility. But balancing that support with my own stability was harder than any spreadsheet.

One message stays with me. The request was reasonable. The amount was not extreme. That was what made it difficult. I read it more than once. I knew the numbers. I knew what the structure could hold. What made the decision hard was not confusion. It was loyalty.

In the end, I sent the sentence I had been avoiding: "Not this month."

The guilt arrived first. The logic came later. But the decision was right. Setting boundaries was not rejection. It was respect for long-term sustainability.

This tension does not fully resolve. Frameworks can make it sound as though the right structure eventually makes these decisions easy. In my experience, they become more clearly reasoned, but not emotionally lighter.

Filipino families—and many immigrant families shaped by collective cultures—do not treat financial support as a transaction. It is part of relationship. When you have more, you share. This is not dysfunction. It is a coherent moral framework, one I was raised inside and one I still believe in.

The difficulty is not the value.

The difficulty is the math.

I have said no to requests I could technically have afforded. I have also said yes when it strained my own system. Neither felt entirely clean. Each required holding two truths: that I love the people I come from, and that I cannot sustain unlimited generosity without damaging the very structure that lets me keep showing up.

The framework does not eliminate the trade-off. What it does is show me more honestly what I am choosing between. "Not this month" leaves room for flow rather than forcing an all-or-nothing break. I do not always get it right. But decisions made from clarity have held up better than those made from guilt or pressure. The guilt does not disappear. The work continues. It simply continues with better information.

Seeing Your Current Money Environment

Before designing supportive community, map your current reality:

Inner circle: List three to five people whose opinions most affect you. For each: Do they support my financial goals, undermine them, or remain neutral?

Support network: List communities you participate in. For each: Does this group reinforce behaviors I'm building?

Environmental inputs: Track media consumption for one week. What money behaviors do these inputs normalize?

Most people discover significant misalignment between financial goals and social context. That's information, not judgment.

Strengthening Your Inner Circle

When you notice mild misalignment—where people respect your goals but don't actively support them—try having explicit values conversations. "Here's what matters to me financially and why." These conversations don't always create agreement, but they often shift the dynamic from assumed judgment to acknowledged difference.

In situations with support potential, ask for specific help rather than hoping people will intuitively understand what you need. "I'm paying off debt aggressively. It would help if you'd be okay with cheaper hangouts and celebrate my milestones." Direct requests make invisible needs visible.

When facing active undermining—where someone consistently pressures you away from your values—the kindest approach to yourself is often setting firm boundaries. "I'm not discussing my financial choices with you anymore because these conversations create stress." This isn't rejection; it's protecting your capacity to stay aligned with what matters.

The trade-off:

What you gain: Reduced daily friction, active support when struggling, celebration of progress, transparency about challenges.

What you give up: Potentially some relationships if they can't adapt, comfort of avoiding hard conversations, ability to keep financial reality completely private.

This may work best when you value authentic relationships over comfortable ones, can tolerate some conversation discomfort, and have enough psychological safety to set boundaries. Move carefully when money boundaries violate deep cultural or family norms, when financial transparency could create safety risks, or when you depend economically on the relationship.

If you're reading this trade-off and feeling the weight of potential relationship loss, that fear is valid and understandable. The question isn't whether it's scary to risk relationships for financial boundaries—it absolutely is. The question is whether the current cost of maintaining those relationships without boundaries is sustainable long-term.

Finding the Right Support Network

When searching for your people, look for communities focused on specific goals. Specificity increases relevance—"debt payoff support" yields better matches than "financial advice."

Before committing, observe whether the culture feels genuinely supportive or quietly competitive. Some groups celebrate others' progress; others create comparison pressure.

Once you find a supportive community, build reciprocity by contributing actively. Offer support to people one step behind you. That exchange makes community sustainable rather than extractive.

Shaping Your Financial Environment

Your media environment shapes what feels normal through constant exposure. Start by systematically unfollowing accounts that trigger spending urges or comparison spirals. Then follow accounts modeling behaviors you're actually building. Replace financial news designed for anxiety with educational content aligned with your goals.

The shift isn't about avoiding all money content—it's about curating inputs that reinforce rather than undermine your values.

Family and Cultural Expectations

Money community isn't just finding supportive people—it's navigating inherited communities whose expectations often conflict with your values.

You might encounter family expectations of financial support, cultural norms around expensive celebrations you can't afford, or pressure toward homeownership when renting serves you better. These conflicts are structural, not personal failures.

Possible approaches:

Partial disclosure without complete transparency. You can set boundaries with explanation: "I can't contribute financially to that celebration, but I can contribute time and presence." Or you can find allies within the culture who share your frustration.

What you can't do: Expect people to change their values because yours changed. You can set boundaries about what you'll do. You can't control whether they understand or approve.

Shared-obligation norms in immigrant families can bring both meaning and pressure, especially when economic realities differ across generations. The tension isn't unique to you. It's structural, built into the gap between cultural expectations formed in one economic context and individual realities in another.

When Support Feels Out of Reach

Some people don't have supportive relationships. Some lack community access due to location, language, disability, or other barriers.

If you're there, that isolation is real. Two things remain true: Online community can partially compensate for geographic isolation. And community building is gradual—you need one connection providing slightly more support than isolation. Then another.

When structural barriers limit community access, seek targeted support. Options include legal aid for documentation or debt disputes, patient advocates for healthcare navigation, caregiver support organizations for respite and resources, and local assistance programs.

Online forums with strong moderation can bridge geographic isolation, while library financial literacy programs and non-profit financial counseling with peer components provide structured entry points.

Community building has its own version of analysis paralysis. If you find yourself researching forums, bookmarking resources, and reading reviews of peer groups without ever sending a single message, you're procrastinating with purpose. One message to one person is worth six months of preparation.

Why Social Context Sustains Change

Everything you've built—the pattern recognition, the nervous system work, the spending systems—exists inside a social context that either supports it or quietly erodes it. Most people don't account for that. They repair their internal relationship with money, then walk back into the same external environment that shaped the problem in the first place.

Family messages helped form your money story. Your cash flow systems survive only if the people around you respect the structure instead of treating it like obsession. Strategic spending holds only if you can withstand the constant social pressure to override your intentional choices.

Community isn't separate from the work you've done. It's the environment that determines whether that work can be sustained.

When your inner circle respects your choices, your support network models behaviors you're building, and your environmental inputs reinforce rather than undermine your goals, maintaining financial discipline becomes dramatically easier. Not because you have more willpower. Because your social context supports rather than resists your choices.

You'll still experience setbacks. Community doesn't eliminate challenges. But it changes how you experience them. A spending slip-up in isolation feels like personal failure. A spending slip-up in a supportive community feels like a normal setback requiring adjustment. That difference determines whether temporary challenges derail progress.

Others' community design doesn't set the template for yours. Someone else's perfect circle of financially aligned friends isn't your benchmark. Design within your reality, not someone else's.

The Work Continues

You've interrupted the pattern and built something substantial. The Loop doesn't disappear, but it no longer has to run by default.

What you've built is not fragile. It includes regulation strong enough to steady you, values clear enough to guide you, structures that redirect money toward what matters, and support that helps the work hold when life gets difficult. That is what makes change sustainable—not perfect execution, but systems that can absorb imperfection.

The work isn't about getting money exactly right. It is about building the capacity to keep choosing toward your values even when circumstances make those choices difficult. That capacity grows through practice, structure, and community, not through isolated willpower.

Six months from now, you'll face unexpected expenses. Someone will pressure you toward spending that doesn't align with your values. You'll have moments of wanting to abandon your systems because maintaining them feels exhausting. That's not failure. That's being human with financial responsibilities in a complex social world.

What's different now is that you have ways to respond. When financial stress activates, you can regulate before reacting. When you're unclear about what matters, you can return to values instead of urgency. When daily spending drifts from intention, you can redirect it. When social pressure pulls you off course, you have language and structure strong enough to protect your choices.

These tools won't make money management effortless. They make it possible. They make it sustainable. They make it yours—designed around your values, adapted to your constraints, and supported by relationships that actually serve you.

The work you are building is gradual and cumulative. It lives in slightly better choices made more often, in returning to your systems after life knocks you off course, in adjusting as circumstances evolve, and in asking for support when you need it.

You are not aiming for financial perfection. You are building financial agency: the capacity to make intentional choices about money based on what genuinely matters to you. Not through one dramatic change, but through accumulated practice. Not through flawless execution, but through persistent return.

How Money Leadership Is Built

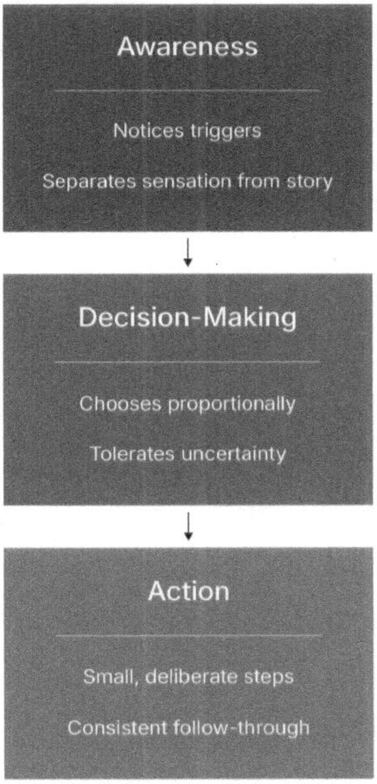

Leadership emerges from repeated clarity.

The work continues. But you do not continue it alone, and you do not continue it without tools.

The next pressure doesn't get to decide what your money means.

Chapter 18: When the Decision Returns

The Loop appeared again recently.

Nothing urgent. A potential investment, familiar options, a decision well within range. Yet within minutes the old pattern stirred — one article leading to another, a comparison spreadsheet opening, another check to ensure nothing had been missed. The content was not the signal. The pattern was.

Years earlier, that quiet expansion would have continued until the decision faded away. This time I saw it clearly: not a need for more information, but the mind's instinctive attempt to eliminate uncertainty before acting. I closed the tabs, wrote the question in plain language, and answered only that.

The choice that followed was not perfect. It did not banish uncertainty. But it was sufficient.

The Smart Struggle Loop does not disappear once you understand it. It continues to surface — in earning, in spending, in investing, in debt, and in the larger decisions that shape a life. It arises whenever intelligence meets uncertainty around money. It will keep arising in different forms.

What changes is not its presence. What changes is its power.

For years, the Loop felt like evidence of failure: that you were behind, that others understood money in ways you never would, that your greatest strength had somehow become your quietest liability.

Now it reads differently.

When the Loop appears, it no longer means you are broken. It means a decision matters. It is your analytical mind trying to protect you, even when that protection is no longer necessary.

You will still face decisions that feel too important to get wrong. You will still encounter uncertainty your mind cannot fully resolve. Analysis will still multiply at times instead of clarifying.

But once you can see the Loop clearly, it stops passing for truth.

You no longer need every unknown resolved before you move. You no longer need to confuse more analysis with more readiness. You no longer need to treat the mind's demand for certainty as proof that certainty is available.

When it shows up in earning, you can recognize anxious scenario-building before it becomes paralysis. When it shows up in spending, you can recognize second-guessing before it becomes avoidance. When it shows up in investing, you can recognize the fantasy that one more week of research will remove the uncertainty markets are built on. When it shows up in debt, you can stop mistaking overthinking for progress. When it shows up in life design, you can stop asking achievement to solve a form of anxiety achievement was never built to solve.

How It All Fits Together

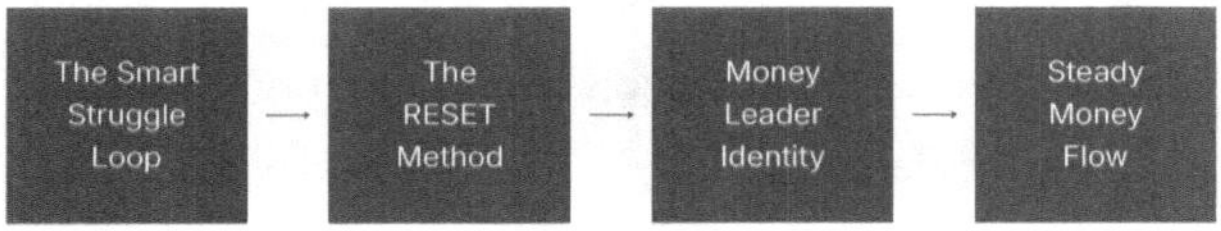

From effort to steadiness.

The Loop had appeared. But this time it was no longer the authority in the room. It was a signal. And the signal meant it was time to decide.

That is the shift. Not that the Loop stops appearing. But that it stops running the decision by default.

You do not escape the Loop.

You lead it.

Epilogue

It is 2:47 a.m. again, or close enough that the body knows the hour.

The phone is in your hand.

The urge is still there. The Loop does not disappear. That was never the promise. The promise was smaller and more true: that the moment would not be over before you were in it.

There is a pause now. Sometimes brief. Sometimes barely noticeable. But real.

Jennifer signed the business loan with hands that still trembled. The trembling was not the point. The point was signing anyway.

Elena cleared her final debt account thirty-six months after she built the spreadsheet she had spent years avoiding. She still hears the old voice sometimes. She has learned to hear it as data.

I still check at midnight sometimes. I catch it faster than I used to. Most of the time.

That is what changes. Not the urge. Not the history money carries. Not the weight of what it meant before you had words for it.

Just this: the pause between the signal and the response. The moment where you are no longer only reacting. The space where something that is actually yours gets to decide.

The work does not finish. It becomes more honestly yours—built from your actual constraints, your examined values, your real capacity, and the life you are actually responsible for. Not the one old scripts taught you to chase.

The numbers will still be there in the morning. So will the questions.

But they no longer arrive as commands.

They arrive as information.

And information, now, can be met.

Not perfectly.

Not without the old weight.

But by you.

Acknowledgement

This book grew out of years of observing how money is rarely just about the numbers.

I am grateful to the professionals who helped bring this manuscript to publication—for the careful attention, visual refinement, and technical support that made the work stronger.

To my family, thank you for your patience, your steady presence, and the space to write.

About the Author

IP Buquiron is the pen name of Isidro Buquiron, a Filipino-Canadian author and professional engineer based in Ontario, Canada. For years, he has observed why intelligent, capable people can remain stuck with money long after they have learned to manage complexity in other areas of life.

His work explores the intersection of money, work, identity, and human behavior, with a focus on recognition over advice, structure over discipline, and clarity without false comfort.

www.ingramcontent.com/pod-product-compliance
Lightning Source LLC
LaVergne TN
LVHW092136071126
851857LV00038BB/461
* 9 7 8 1 0 6 9 4 5 9 1 5 2 *